MUSIC IN POLAND

LUDWIK ERHARDT

MUSIC IN POLAND

INTERPRESS PUBLISHERS
WARSAW 1975

Cover design:
JERZY KĘPKIEWICZ

Polish editor:
WANDA MICHALAK

Make-up editor:
LUCYNA DUKAJ

Translated by:
JAN ALEKSANDROWICZ

Photos:
ANDRZEJ ZBORSKI

This is the one thousand four hundred and twenty-fourth publication
of Interpress publishers
This book also appears in Polish, French, German, Italian and Spanish

PRINTED IN POLAND

RSW „PRASA—KSIĄŻKA—RUCH", ZAKŁADY GRAFICZNE W ŁODZI

TABLE OF CONTENTS

The world knows little about Polish music. Chopin and Paderewski are household names and some may have heard of Moniuszko and Szymanowski, but that tends to be that — not only in the case of the averagely educated man, but even of the knowledgeable concert-goer. Moreover it was, until recently, about all the information to be found in music histories and encyclopaedias published in other countries. The first breach was made by the fifth edition of Grove's Dictionary of Music and Musicians (1954) whose nine volumes contained a considerable amount of material on Polish music. Then came the comprehensive and scholarly articles in the monumental Die Musik in Geschichte und Gegenwart (1949—68), and the successive and continually supplemented editions of Riemann's Musiklexikon. There have also been a number of publications — most of them now out of print — by Polish musicologists issued in foreign languages for the benefit of readers abroad. As a result people with a professional interest in music are now better informed both about the work of contemporary composers and the history of Polish music. Apart from the strenuous international efforts of Polish musicologists, an important role has been played by two major music festivals: the "Warsaw Autumn" International Festival of Contemporary Music, organized annually since 1956, and the Bydgoszcz Music Festival, inaugurated in 1963 and devoted primarily to old music and reviving Polish works for an international audience. The latter, also designed to serve music scholarship, is usually accompanied by symposia or even congresses. Every third year, it is called Musica Antiqua Europae Orientalis and makes for an interesting juxtaposition of the Polish achievement with the rest of Eastern and Central Europe's. Nevertheless the fact remains that for the broad public, Poland's share in the development of European music compared with Italy, Germany, Russia or France seems more or less infinitesimal.

My object in these pages is to redress this traditional image. Not, of course by trying to convince the reader that Poland produced composers greater than Okeghem, Monteverdi, Bach and Mozart, but only by demonstrating that Polish music did not start with Chopin and that it had many noteworthy composers before him whom only the misfortunes of our history thrust into oblivion. For it was in the 19th century that the tide of musical antiquarianism rose, and that was a time when Poland had disappeared from the political map, partitioned between three powers which did everything to belittle her contribution to European culture, a compaign pursued most ruthlessly in Germany, the very country in which the new discipline of musicology emerged. As a result the picture created and perpetuated of the history of European music was one in which Poland was virtually non-existent. The attempts of the first — and for that matter few — Polish musicologists (Aleksander Poliński, Henryk Opieński, Adolf Chybiński, Zdzisław Jachimecki, Józef Reiss), to set the record straight were of no avail; prior to and after World War I they made many sensational discoveries, but a thorough investigation of the history of music in Poland was a task for several generations and could only be accomplished by their pupils.

World War I wreaked havoc enough, but it was nothing compared to World War II: libraries were burned down, collections piecemealed, antiquities pillaged and destroyed, and the people who could study and evaluate them, killed. In the mid-fifties, however, a new and post-war trained generation of Polish musicologists set about the arduous assignment of taking stock of our assets in the field of the history of music — such as had been spared by the war — a task for which in the inter-war period there had been neither the people nor the money. A systematic and increasingly wide-ranging programme, financed by the State and master-minded by Professor Hieronim Feicht (1894—1967), began to yield unexpected results: dreadful as the losses were found to be, material whose existence had never been so much as suspected was unearthed in old archives and monastic libraries, which shook many of the accepted views of the history of Polish music. As a result the picture which emerges, though still sketchy and by no means definitive, is far richer than the existing literature would suggest.

I. POLISH MUSIC BEFORE CHOPIN

The Middle Ages; the Renaissance — the Golden Age of Polish Culture; Music Yields to Fire and Sword; in the Shadow of Rationalism

From the earliest times, music performed the same function in Poland as in other European countries, and was dependent on economic and political circumstances. Its history began in the 10th century when Poland was organized into a strong state and, through official adoption of the Christian religion (in 966), entered the orbit of European civilization. But to judge by the references made by travellers and the oldest chroniclers a native music culture had evolved much earlier. The interesting process of its collision with the Gregorian chorale imported together with Chrstianity can only be reconstructed hypothetically. The earliest extant scores date from the middle of the 11th century and bear witness to the cultivation of advanced forms of plainsong. The number of manuscripts from this period is quite appreciable (over 400 items), the research of the past few years having been particularly fruitful and resulting in the revision of previous views of the history of Polish medieval music; it is now clear that it developed rigorously and was in close touch with the main European centres. This was undoubtedly connected with the rising power of Poland as a state which had grown in strength under the Piast dynasty, in spite of numerous wars, and at the end of the 14th century, when the first of the Jagiellon kings ascended the throne, was approaching the apogee of its might.

Among the medieval scores which have survived intact the most noteworthy is *Bogurodzica* (The Mother of God), a monodic hymn by an anonymous 13th-century author, the oldest composition we know of with a Polish text (most were still in Latin). Its musical and poetic values and its majestic strain of chivalry made it for several centuries the favourite song of the Polish knighthood and the equivalent of a national anthem; to this day it remains the only work of old Polish music to be generally known. The outstanding composer of this era was Mikołaj of Radom, active at the beginning of the 15th century, whose polyphonic works (e.g. *Magnificat, Hystoriographi aciem mentis)*, show, apart from their artistic quality, technical mastery unusual for those days and are evidence that Polish music was then on a par with that of the greatest centres of western Europe.

The heyday of Polish culture and of Polish music came during the Renaissance. Under the Jagiellons Poland grew into a vast and powerful kingdom which attracted artists and scholars from all over the world. Cracow, its capital, became one of Europe's main cultural centres. It was there in the second half of the 15th century that the great sculptor Wit Stwosz carved the famous altar-piece in St. Mary's Church and other masterpieces. In the 16th century, Italian artists streamed in at the invitation of Sigismund I's wife, the influential Bona Sforza (1494—1557), a daughter of the

Duke of Milan. Cracow's University, founded in 1364, had by the 15th century acquired a fame which eclipsed all other institutions of higher learning in this part of Europe. It was also an important nursery of music. The most important role, however, was played by the orchestra and choir maintained by the king, which was directed by accomplished Polish and foreign musicians and performed works by the best composers of the day. In the middle of the 16th century there was founded another choir for the special purpose of singing at services in the cathedral of Wawel Castle in Cracow. Music-printing also flourished, thanks mainly to the dissenters who found refuge in Cracow under the enlightened and tolerant rule of the Jagiellons. Music throve outside Cracow as well, in the palaces of the magnates who followed the example of the royal court by similar patronage of the arts.

Most of the medieval music still extant is religious, although we know from chronicles and other records that there had already sprung up a strong current of secular music — chansons de geste, court music, the ballads and dances of strolling players — and by the beginning of the 14th century, musicians' guilds were being formed. Of the works preserved the most noteworthy are the Cracow students' comic *Breve regnum*, and the hymn *Cracovia civitas*.

The Renaissance, on the other hand, bequeathed a much more varied heritage: vocal and instrumental works, organ compositions and dances, polyphonic secular music and superb oratorios and masses. No longer were the composers anonymous as they had mainly been in the Middle Ages and some of their biographies are even known in detail.

The finest extant example of Polish 16th-century

music is probably *Melodies for a Polish Psalter* by Mikołaj Gomółka (c. 1535—93), who worked in Cracow and Sandomierz. Printed in Cracow in 1580, it is a sequence of 150 polyphonic psalms *a capella*, set to verse translations by the great Renaissance poet, Jan Kochanowski. The composer's dedication indicates that they were not intended for trained musicians but for performance within the family circle. As a result they are fairly simple technically, but compensate by possessing lively rhythms, sometimes of a dance character, containing illustrative and programme elements, abounding in harmonic phrases of considerable boldness for those times and, most notably, displaying a striking melodic invention of a distinctly individual character.

For a greater degree of technical sophistication we must look to Marcin Leopolita (d. 1589) and Wacław of Szamotuły (c. 1526—60), musicians connected with the royal court in Cracow. The former is the author of the consummate five-voice *Missa paschalis*, the earliest of the complete Masses *a cappella* in Polish music preserved in full, Wacław of Szamotuły of polyphonic songs (e.g. *It's Growing Dusk*) and motets (e.g. *In te Domine speravi* or *Ego sum pastor bonus)*, which were so highly thought of as to be included in foreign collections of the times alongside works by composers of the calibre of Josquin des Prés, Orlando di Lasso, or Nicolas Gombert. Further evidence of the high standard attained by music in Poland is the *Tablature* of Jan of Lublin, dating from the first half of the 16th century, the most comprehensive of all known European organ tablatures of that period, which contains several Polish pieces as well as the considerable number by distinguished Netherland, German, Italian and French Renaissance composers.

Instrumental and dance music also throve. Among the Polish and foreign lute-players and composers active in Poland in the second half of the 16th century were Valentin Greff-Bakfark (1507—76), Wojciech Długoraj (1558—1619), Jakub Polak (Jacob Polonais, 1545—1605) and Diomedes Cato (c. 1570—1615). An organist of great repute was Jakub Wolski. The extant organ tablatures with Polish and foreign works show it to be a field of equally substantial accomplishment.

At the turn of the 16th and 17th centuries a number of excellent violin makers, Bartłomiej Kiejcher, Marcin Groblicz (the elder) and Baltazar Dankwart, were producing instruments valued as highly as those of Maggini of Brescia. The references to "Polish violins" in the writings of Martin Agricola, the German theorist of the 16th century, and Michael Praetorius from the early 17th century, are still something of a tantalizing mystery: no works written for this instrument have survived, but it must be inferred from the descriptions given in these works that they were very popular in Poland. The most interesting thing is that Agricola makes it clear that in design and the manner of playing these "Polish violins" differed considerably from the widespread Renaissance violas of Italian origin and, if anything, resembled the Baroque violins from which the modern instrument evolved. This has led some historians to put forward the hypothesis that they were in fact the original prototype. Be that as it may, they were a secular, or maybe even a folk, instrument used for accompanying dances. Of this sort of music, widely cultivated though it was by all social classes during the Renaissance, we know paradoxically little, no doubt because, being an applied art with no higher aspirations, it was recorded neither in writing or print but handed down from generation to generation. Only a few Polish dances have survived in organ transcriptions, but together with the many written descriptions they give us some idea of the wealth of the native dances in fashion at the court, among the nobles, gentry and burghers, and probably in the countryside as well. They must have had a specifically national character since numerous foreign collections from the 16th and 17th century contain such terms as *chorea polonica, balletto polacco*, etc. Moreover, in the second half of the 16th century, Italian and, later, French dances spread widely in Poland in the wake of animated international contacts.

The 16th century, called the "Golden Age" of Polish music, saw a brilliant explosion in all fields of art and learning and the Renaissance developed a momentum which carried far into the 17th century, despite the country's steadily worsening fortunes, and was due to European humanism reaching Poland when she was at the height of her political power and blending with two specific features of her history in this period: religious tolerance and a system of democracy which, albeit confined to the landed gentry, was a check to absolutism. Towards the end of the 16th century, however, a rot began to set in and gradually grew until it eventually brought Poland to ruin. The outward symptoms of these brewing political problems were the adoption of an elective monarchy after the death without issue of the last of the powerful Jagiellon kings (1572), a measure which, though apparently consistent with the principle of a democracy of the whole gentry, in reality plunged the country into political strife and increasingly made the king's authority dependent on the great nobles and their feuds; it also opened the way to intrigues by foreign powers seeking to gain possession of the Polish throne.

A series of concessions to the Church made by succeeding kings in their bids for election resulted in the ascendancy of Counter-reformation in the 17th century. Though the excesses of wars of religion and persecutions were avoided, the tolerant spirit of Renaissance humanism was swallowed up in the ideology of the all-powerful Jesuits. Last but not least, the vast dominions amassed by the Jagiellons became increasingly exposed to the depredations of neighbours now growing in power and bent on profiting from the weaknesses beginning to sap a country whose favours they had until then been so happy to court. An answer to these threats was sought in dynastic alliances: the first elected king was Henri de Valois, the future Henry III of France. After his brief and unfortunate reign, the throne passed to the Prince of Transylvania, Stephen Batory, and upon his death (1586), Poland was ruled for eighty years by kings of the Swedish Vasa dynasty. The idea of political union with Sweden collapsed, however, when Swedish opposition led to Sigismund III Vasa being deposed in Sweden and embroiled Poland in gruelling wars which went on for almost the whole of the 17th century. Though the havoc wreaked by them was immense they turned out, paradoxically enough, to be the saving of part of our cultural heritage. The Swedish invaders plundered mercilessly, but their spoils eventually found their way into libraries and museums in Sweden and are now records all the more priceless for the huge number of antiquities lost forever in the pillage and devastation suffered by Poland in the past three centuries.

The second half of the 17th century was a series of wars with Russia and Turkey. In 1683, King John III Sobieski gained his famous victory over the Turkish army besieging Vienna, thereby putting an end to Turkish expansion in Europe. But despite military successes, the unending wars of the 17th century were economically ruinous and spread the seeds of anarchy. Though her frontiers were still far-flung Poland entered the 18th century almost on her last legs, with Russia, Prussia and Austria all scheming her destruction. Under the camouflage of alliances, the thought of carving up this rich territory quickly evolved into a primary political goal.

This cursory delve into history was necessary to set the background for cultural developments and for the history of our music in the period that followed the Renaissance "Golden Age". Otherwise it would perhaps be difficult to understand the gradual decline that began in the 17th century and the reasons that prevented composers of notable gifts (and such, after all, there were) becoming known in Europe. The simple fact is that Poland was slowly sinking into obscurity and, as a result, less and less was heard of her artists. It was nevertheless a gradual process. As late as 1611 the collected compositions of Mikołaj Zieleński, organist and conductor of Primate Wojciech Baranowski's orchestra in Łowicz, were issued in Venice. Its two parts were called *Offertoria totius anni* and *Communiones totius anni,* and contained 121 different vocal and instrumental works representing the nascent Baroque polychoral style. We know little about the author of these works, which are of exceptional beauty and a tribute to the degree of virtuosity attained in composition in Poland during the late Renaissance and early Baroque.

That they were published in Venice seems to show that their quality was not lost on the contemporary public.

At the beginning of the 17th century, many gifted Italian composers were active in Poland, mainly in Warsaw whither King Sigismund III Vasa had moved the royal court in 1596 in order to be closer to Sweden and created a new and strong cultural centre. Among those who spent some length of time in Warsaw were Luca Marenzio, Annibale Stabile and Tarquinio Merula. An excellent royal orchestra was directed by Asprilio Pacelli, Giovanni Francesco Anerio, Marco Scacchi, and, later, Bartłomiej Pękiel and Jacek Różycki. It performed in Warsaw throughout the 17th century until Augustus II of Saxony was elected to the Polish throne and transferred it in 1697 to his permanent seat in Dresden.

Opera also fared well at the royal castle, the first such theatre outside Italy being founded in Warsaw by King Ladislaus IV, the second ruler of the Vasa dynasty. In 1628, an Italian company appeared in a production about which we unfortunately know little more than the title, *Galatea,* the same being true of the ten other operas and ballets presented up to 1646 when the Swedish wars and the depleted state of the royal exchequer brought such performances to an end. On the other hand, the influence and wealth of the great nobles had been rising so steadily since the 16th century that they were eager to outdo the royal court in splendour. Disastrous as the economic consequences were, such rivalry offered an exceptional chance to artists and musicians in times that were growing increasingly hard. For example, Stanisław Lubomirski had his own opera theatre at Wiśnicz by the beginning of the 17th century, and numerous companies of musicians were maintained by Krzysztof Radziwiłł and Janusz Tyszkiewicz in Vilna, Mikołaj Wolski at Krzepice, and many other grandees. Of a particularly high standard were the orchestras of the Primate in Łowicz and of other prelates in Gniezno, Lvov, Wrocław and Płock. A large number were also attached to cathedrals, collegiate churches and monasteries, and though the players might not be as good as the magnates', they reached a much wider audience.

It was chiefly the mass of the lesser gentry and the townsmen who were hit by the gradual decline in Poland's political stature and the deepening economic malaise which accompanied it. The 17th century saw Poland degenerate into a country of increasingly glaring contrasts — to quote the distinguished historian, Professor Władysław Tomkiewicz — "of ostentatious wealth and gross poverty, gorgeous apparel and appalling dirt, orthodoxy and belief in witchcraft and sorcery, universal ignorance and a sprinkling of intellectual refinement among individuals or even communities (e.g. Gdańsk); Stanisław Herakliusz Lubomirski was capable of being both a bigot and a religious sceptic, a high-living libertine and an elegant aesthete. For lack of a royal court in the capital (John III and the Saxon kings spent little time in Warsaw) to co-ordinate culture there sprang up a great many minor centres which resulted in a decline in its general standard but also made for great differentiation."

Against this background it is easier to understand why Polish music failed in the Baroque period, after having developed so splendidly in the preceding centuries, to produce artists of the calibre of Monteverdi,

Bach or Haendel. Considering the circumstances, however, what vigour and creative potential it did possess can only be admired.

The list of Polish composers is a very long one, and here there is room only for the most prominent. Chief among them was Bartłomiej Pękiel (d. 1670), active in Warsaw and in Cracow, of whose numerous works the greatest are: *Audite mortales,* a magnificent oratorio on the Last Judgment, for six voices and instrumentalists, and *Missa pulcherrima,* universally considered the finest *a capella* Mass in Polish music. It is Marcin Mielczewski (c. 1600—51), a member of the royal orchestra and later in charge of one in Płock, the author of more than 50 instrumental and vocal works in the concertante style (including *Vesperae Dominicales* for solo voices, choir and instrumentalists), who seems, however, to have enjoyed the highest degree of contemporary recognition; he was published in Venice and Berlin, and manuscripts can be found in Czechoslovakia, France and Germany. A testimonial to the high standard of instrumental music are the works of Adam Jarzębski (c. 1590—1649), a violinist, architect and poet active first in Berlin and then in Warsaw. His *Canzoni e Concerti* are akin in harmony and form to contemporary Italian music (Frescobaldi) and unquestionably ahead of the German or French music of this period. Instrumental works were also composed by Mielczewski (*Canzoni*), Pękiel (dances for lute), Andrzej Rohaczewski (*Canzona a 4*), and Stanisław Sylwester Szarzyński (*Sonata a 3*). The latter, a Cistercian monk, is one of the most obscure figures in the history of Polish music; all we know about him is that his floruit came at the end of the 17th century and that his works included several very interesting still extant vocal-and-instrumental concertos (e.g. *Jesu, spes mea,* for soprano, two violins and organ, or *Pariendo non gravaris,* for tenor, two violins, viola and organ). The most creative talent in Polish Baroque music appears, however, to have been Grzegorz Gerwazy Gorczycki (c. 1667—1734), conductor of the cathedral orchestra in Cracow. Especially noteworthy are his motets for solo voices, choir and orchestra *(Illuxit sol* or *Laetatus sum)* and, still more, *Completorium,* a cycle of psalms and songs for choir, two violins, trumpets and figured bass, a concertante of great technical accomplishment, invention and glow, compared — not without reason — to Haendel. He was probably also the author of the first symphonic composition in Polish music, *Overture,* the score of which has unfortunately been lost.

Profuse and relatively detailed though our knowledge of Polish Baroque music is, there are numerous gaps. One of the biggest is solo instrumental music, especially for organ. Until recently, we knew of only one organ work by a Polish composer of the 17th century: the very interesting *Prelude* by Jan Podbielski. Only in the past few years have other works been discovered: by Andrzej Rohaczewski, organist at Albrecht Radziwiłł's court at Ołyka and Nieśwież *(Canzona a 4),* Piotr Żelechowski *(Fantasia)* and Bartłomiej Pękiel's *Fugue.* These four and a few anonymous ones represent all that has survived to our days from the undoubtedly copious Polish organ music of the 17th century. It must, however, have attained a high artistic standard since such outstanding composers as Zieleński and Pękiel were both organists and many others enjoyed a reputation as excellent virtuosi. Some of them were pupils of Girolamo Frescobaldi; Andrzej Niżankowski and Andrzej Chyliński were for some time employed as organists in Rome and Padua; Michał Cracovita was active in Copenhagen, many Polish organists visited Bohemia, and in Poland itself Adam Mosiążek, Jan Schmidt and Kasper Bystrzycki were among players famed for their virtuosity.

The long roster of Polish 17th century organists shows that such music was very popular, so that it is a real misfortune that the manuscript organ tablature discovered a few years ago in Pelplin and dating to about 1620, one of the most comprehensive written records of its kind in the world (911 pieces), contains extremely few original Polish compositions. However, 17th-century organ music is another subject where there are still many loose ends for the historians to tie up.

During the first half of the 18th century Poland was ruled by Saxon kings of the Wettin line. Economic ruin and externally fomented anarchy were accompanied by a relentless relapse into backwardness and a wave of religious fanaticism, in sorry contrast to the rationalist currents taking hold of western European minds. At the same time men of the political calibre of Peter the Great in Russia and Frederick William I in Prussia came to power in the hostile states across her borders. The Treaty of Loewenwold in 1732 definitively laid down the guiding principles of the policy of Austria, Prussia and Russia towards Poland, including the possibility of armed intervention should a royal election take a turn not to their liking. Fearing a revival of Poland's former power, they paralyzed by political artifice all attempts at reform and emancipation. Nevertheless in the middle of the 18th century, the spirit of reform began to prevail. Its adherents aligned themselves with the artistocratic Czartoryski family to form a strong political party urging changes in the system of government, the law, the economy and education. Its programme was taken up by Poland's last king, the enlightened Stanislaus Augustus Poniatowski (1764—95). By means of a shaky alliance with Russia he tried to manoeuvre a way through the growing internal and external difficulties. Things, however, had gone too far for even so deft a politician to succeed. In 1772, Prussia, Russia and Austria banded together to carry out the first Partition, seizing 30 per cent of Poland's territory. Twenty years later came the second Partition despite armed resistance, and the kingdom was reduced to a third of its former area. In 1795, after the defeat of the insurrection led by Tadeusz Kościuszko, the dismemberment was made complete, Poniatowski was forced to abdicate, and Poland was wiped off the map of Europe for more than a hundred years.

Stanislaus Augustus' 30-year reign was a singular period in the history of Polish culture and so came to bear his name. The obscurantism of the Saxon age was swept away by an explosive tide of rationalism and there began an efflorescence of political thought, learning and art comparable only to the "Golden Age" of the Renaissance and nursed by the efforts of enlightened individuals, the Czartoryski party, and the king himself. Fully aware of the hopelessness of Poland's political situation, he concentrated on internal matters, social reforms, and economic and intellectual progress, and placed his hopes for the restoration of the country's greatness above all on its youth. Royal patronage brought about a remarkable upsurge in nearly all fields of art, most notable in literature, theatre, architecture and painting.

After the final Partition, Stanisław Staszic, one of

the wisest men of that time, observed that "even a great nation may fall, only a base one decays". For the idea of staving off brute force by fostering the spiritual values of society had during the Stanislaus period been turned into a distinctively Polish raison d'état and passed on to the upcoming Romantic generation. In this design music was, however, probably the least conspicuous element. Partly because it was of little interest to the king, partly because it then lacked the fibre to measure up to the social and educational challenges set before art. The end of the 17th century and the subsequent Saxon period, with the Jesuits tightening their grip to a stranglehold and a fanatical allegiance to catholicism becoming rampant, had resulted in a hegemony of sacred music. As a result the symphonic and operatic forms which surfaced in the Stanislaus period had too frail a foundation — and may also have lacked composers good enough.

The research of the past few years has increased considerably our stock of 18th-century music. The earliest Polish symphonies we know of were written by Jakub Gołąbek (1739—89), a Cracow composer of cantatas, Masses and motets. These resemble the early symphonies of Haydn; so, for that matter, do works by Antoni Milwid, Wojciech Dankowski or Jan Wański (1762—1800). The last of these lived mainly in Poznań, and wrote Masses and operas; in his extant symphonic compositions the influence of Polish folk music can already be detected. Symphonies by A. Haczewski, Karol Pietrowski and Bazyli Bohdanowicz are interesting attempts to emphasize a distinct national character by introducing the rhythms of such dances as the polonaise and the cracovienne. The greatest names among Polish composers of the classical period were made, however, by two violinists: Jan Kleczyński (1756—1828), who worked in Vienna from 1803 as conductor of the court orchestra and published all his works there, and Feliks Janiewicz (1762—1848), a pupil of Haydn and a violinist at King Stanislaus Augustus' court in Warsaw, who settled in Britain in 1792 and was one of the founders of the Royal Philharmonic Society and the Edinburgh festivals of music.

While the number of symphonies, overtures, chamber and solo compositions, written in Poland in the second half of the 18th century, is by no means negligible, everything indicates that the chief current of the Stanislaus period was opera. Monopolized as it was by Italian and German artists, it had not in Saxon times been popular with the Polish public. The creation of a native repertoire, at first based on Italian models, was eventually attempted in the middle of the 18th century in the private theatres of the nobles, above all the Radziwiłłs' at Nieśwież, the Ogińskis' at Słonim, and the Czartoryskis' at Puławy. Of the many operas and vaudevilles that were composed as a result by such individuals as Michał Kazimierz Ogiński (1728—1800), Jan Dawid Holland (1746—1827), and Franciszek Lessel (1780—1838), only fragments have survived. A much wider degree of interest followed the opening by Wojciech Bogusławski in Warsaw in 1765 of Poland's first professional theatre, where opera soon joined drama among the productions. In many cases these were adaptations, and included the early works of Mozart which were presented in Warsaw soon after their premières in Vienna. Gradually, however, Polish composers were added to the repertoire. The first was a vaudeville, *Nędza uszczęśliwiona* (Misery Made Happy), by Maciej Kamieński (1734—1821), which was staged in 1778 and was the first of his many successes. Operas were also written by Jan Dawid Holland, Antoni Wejnert (1751—1850), and Joachim Albertini (1751—1811). All in all, between 1778 and 1794, Bogusławski's theatre produced some thirty operas composed in Poland but on the Italian model. The turning point was the vaudeville, *Cud mniemany czyli Krakowiacy i Górale* (The Seeming Miracle or Cracovians and Highlanders) by Jan Stefani (1746—1829), in which Polish folk tunes and dances were used for the first time on a larger scale. This work was a huge triumph, giving rise to a national strain of opera. The Partitions, however, made it increasingly difficult to continue.

Polish music — and Polish culture as a whole — now entered on the most daunting period in their history, one in which artists were forced perhaps for the first time to use their pens and brushes as weapons in a struggle for political freedom.

RECORDINGS BY "POLSKIE NAGRANIA — MUZA" OF OLD POLISH MUSIC (selection)

The Musica Antiqua Polonica Series:

Vocal Music of the Middle Ages (Latin religious and secular monody, Polish religious monody, Latin polyphony)
    Choir of the Polish Radio in Wrocław, conducted by Stanisław Krukowski. XL 0578

Origins of Polish Music (anonymous composers, Jędrzej Gałka, Ładysław of Gielniów, Mikołaj of Radom)
    Soloists, Boys' and Men's Choir of the Pomeranian Philharmonic, Capella Bydgostiensis pro Musica Antiqua, conducted by Stanisław Gałoński. XL 0294

Music in Wawel Castle (Mikołaj of Radom, Mikołaj of Cracow, Wacław of Szamotuły, Mikołaj of Chrzanów, Diomedes Cato, Marcin Leopolita, Krzysztof Klabon)
    Madrigal Singers, Capella Bydgostiensis pro Musica Antiqua, conducted by Stanisław Gałoński. XL 0296

Mikołaj Gomółka: *Melodies for a Polish Psalter* (selection)
    Boys' and Men's Choir of the Poznań Philharmonic, conducted by Stefan Stuligrosz. XL 0234

Music of Warsaw Castle (Marco Scacchi, Marcin Mielczewski, Bartłomiej Pękiel, Wojciech Długoraj, Diomedes Cato, Adam Jarzębski, Jacek Różycki)
    Musicae Antiquae Collegium Varsoviense, conducted by Stefan Sutkowski. XL 0295

Italian Composers in Poland (Luca Marenzio, Giovanni B. Cocciola, Asprilio Pacelli, Diomedes Cato, Tarquinio Merula, Marcello di Capua)
    Capella Bydgostiensis pro Musica Antiqua, conducted by Stanisław Gałoński, Madrigal Singers, Musicae Antiquae Collegium Varsoviense,, conducted by Stefan Sutkowski. XL 0537

Mikołaj Zieleński: *Offertoria, Magnificat, Communiones*
    Capella Bydgostiensis pro Musica Antiqua, conducted by Sta-

nisław Gałoński, Choir of the Polish Radio in Wrocław, conducted by Edmund Kajdasz. XL 0302

Dances, Songs and Pavans from the 17th Century
Eugeniusz Sąsiadek (tenor), Fistulatores et Tubicinatores Varsovienses, conducted by Kazimierz Piwkowski. XL 0612.

Polish Instrumental Music of the 17th Century (Mikołaj Zieleński, Adam Jastrzębski and Marcin Mielczewski)
The "Con moto ma cantabile" Ensemble, conducted by Tadeusz Ochlewski. XL 0303

Instrumental Music of the Polish Baroque (Adam Jarzębski and Marcin Mielczewski)
The Chamber Ensemble of the National Philharmonic, conducted by Karol Teutsch. XL 0200

Polish Organ Music of the 16th and 17th Centuries (anonymous composers, Piotr Żelichowski, Jakub Sowa, Mikołaj of Cracow, Diomedes Cato, Marcin Leopolita, Jan Podbielski, Andrzej Rohaczewski)
Joachim Grubich, organ. XL 0235

Marcin Leopolita: *Missa paschalis;* Bartłomiej Pękiel: *Missa pulcherrima*
Choir of the Polish Radio in Wrocław, conducted by Edmund Kajdasz. XL 0188

Franciszek Lilius, Marcin Mielczewski, Stanisław Sylwester Szarzyński, Mikołaj Zieleński: Vocal and Instrumental Works
Men's choir and instrumental ensemble of the Polish Radio in Wrocław, conducted by Edmund Kajdasz. XL 0548

Marcin Mielczewski: *Vesperae Dominicales*
The choir and chamber orchestra of the Polish Radio in Wrocław, conducted by Edmund Kajdasz. XL 0358

Stanisław Sylwester Szarzyński: Vocal and Instrumental Concertos
Soloists, Musicae Antiquae Collegium Varsoviense, conducted by Jerzy Dobrzański. XL 0524

Music in Old Cracow (Grzegorz Gerwazy Gorczycki, Wincenty Maxylewicz, Franciszek Lilius, J. Staromieyski)

The choir and chamber orchestra of the Polish Radio in Wrocław, conducted by Edmund Kajdasz. XL 0368

Grzegorz Gerwazy Gorczycki: *Completorium, Missa paschalis* Capella Bydgostiensis pro Musica Antiqua, conducted by Stanisław Gałoński, Choir of the Polish Radio in Wrocław, conducted by Edmund Kajdasz. XL 0277

Harpsichord Music of the 16th—18th Centuries (anonymous composers, Wojciech Długoraj, Jakub Polak, Jan Podbielski, Bazyli Bohdanowicz, Józef Kozłowski, Michał Kleofas Ogiński) Barbara Strzelecka, harpsichord. XL 0614

Marcin Józef Żebrowski: *Magnificat.* Józef Kobierkiewicz: *Ego Mater Pulchrae Dilectionis* Soloists, Madrigal Singers, the Warsaw Chamber Orchestra, Musicae Antiquae Collegium Varsoviense, conducted by Jerzy Dobrzański. XL 0496

Mateusz Zwierzchowski: *Requiem* Soloists, choir and orchestra of the Pomeranian Philharmonnic, conducted by Zbigniew Chwedczuk. XL 0275

Józef Zeidler: *Vespers* Soloists, choir and orchestra of the Pomeranian Philharmonnic, conducted by Zbigniew Chwedczuk. XL 0289

Polish Symphonies of the 18th Century (A. Haczewski, Karol Pietrowski, Bazyli Bohdanowicz) The Poznań Chamber Orchestra, conducted by Robert Satanowski. XL 0523

Jakub Gołąbek: Three Symphonies. The Poznań Philharmonic Chamber Orchestra, conducted by Robert Satanowski. XL 0288

Polish Music of the Age of Enlightenment (Paweł Sieprawski, Feliks Janiewicz, Jan Dawid Holland, J. Staromieyski, Maciej Radziwiłł) The "Con Moto ma Cantabile" Ensemble, conducted by Tadeusz Ochlewski. XL 0507

Jan Wański: Two Symphonies Poznań Philharmonic Orchestra, conducted by Robert Satanowski. XL 0194

II. POLISH MUSIC IN THE YEARS OF NATIONAL SERVITUDE

The Hopes and Setbacks of the Generation of Romantics; Chopin: His Artistic Lineage, Life and Work; Moniuszko: Music Against De-nationalization; Great Virtuosi; Henryk Wieniawski; Folk Music Collections and Research; Oskar Koberg; A Gloomy Fin-de-Siècle

Though the subject of this book is music, the history of any field of Polish culture is so closely intertwined with the history of the nation that without some knowledge of the latter, the names of composers and artistic events will seem to form a fortuitous and baffling mosaic with no apparent organizing principle or logical pattern. This is particularly true of the 19th century. Its course was as stormy for the Polish people as for other European nations, but it had in addition certain specific features which affected its state of mind fundamentally. For this, be it remembered, was a century of servitude, of insurrections and defeats, of surges of hope and plunges into despair, all of which had a decisive impact on all aspects of Polish life. Only ten years after it was lost, independence seemed about to be restored in the wake of the Napoleonic wars. Polish patriots believed in Napoleon and the younger ones eagerly enlisted under his banners in the hope of redeeming their country's freedom with their blood. Though nothing came of these expectations the next generation was not disheartened. Fired by the spirit of Romanticism and encouraged by the revolutionary move-

ERRATA

Page	Line	For	Read
6	2nd from top	TEMPT..........	TEMPT...... 74
6	11th from top	V. IN THE VAN OF WORLD MU-SIC...... 10	V. IN THE VAN OF WORLD MU-SIC...... 104
6	3rd from bottom	OF NEWEST PO-LISH MUSIC (se-lection)...... 15	OF NEWEST PO-LISH MUSIC (se-lection)...... 159
12th page of photographs between pp. 96 and 97.	Caption top right	(K. H. Wörner) – "a modern compo-ser [who writes] mo-dern beautiful mu-sic" Tadeusz Baird-one of the initiators of the "Warsaw Autumn" Festivals	Tadeusz Baird – "a modern composer [who writes] modern beautiful music" (K. H. Wörner), one of the initia-tors of the "War-saw Autumn" Fe-stivals

ments in Europe, they took to arms in the November Rising of 1830. Bloodily though it was suppressed by Tsarist troops, a whole series of local rebellions and conspiracies continued to shake Poland almost unceasingly, culminating in 1863 in the January Rising, the last nationwide but again abortive upheaval.

These armed bids for freedom had manifold consequences: a number of social reforms and consolidation of the sense of national identity, on the one hand, exacerbation of the relations between the partitioning powers and the Polish people, on the other. Within less than forty years, the Russian liberalism of Tsar Alexander I had turned into the savage reign of terror of Alexander II who, in concert with Austria and Prussia, stamped out the least hint of patriotic stirrings and was bent on de-nationalizing the Polish people. These persecutions drove many — the young in particular — into exile, the cream of the nation preferring to seek refuge abroad where they formed politically and artistically dynamic centres, mainly in France. In Poland intellectual and economic life fell into decay, reducing her to one of Europe's backwaters, and recovery of independence and revival of bygone glories became more a matter of faith than a real prospect.

The country's pauperization from top to bottom and sense of helplessness against brute force had an overpowering effect on the mood of society: the youthful, Romantic elation of the first half of the 19th century, nurtured in the 18th-century ideological soil of the Stanislaus period and subsequently fanned by the spell of the Napoleonic myth was deflated in the second half by the succession of tragic setbacks into a sceptical attitude towards the idea of armed revolt. In its place came the notion of advancing the cause through political realism and social reconstruction based on re-invigoration of economic and cultural endeavour. In music these two attitudes found their fullest reflection in the figures, respectively, of Chopin and Moniuszko.

Polish music of the 19th century — or at least its image for subsequent generations — was so dominated by these two very different composers that all other creative endeavour was quite overshadowed. It is hard therefore to resist a picture of both of them, and Chopin in particular, dropping right out of the blue like some *deus ex machina* and having no artistic genealogy or tradition behind them. Such an impression would be totally false. The turn of the 18th and 19th century, the prelude to Chopin's appearance, was a very fruitful time for music, abounding in composers whose only fault was to be eclipsed by his genius. Warsaw was the main musical centre, though a pale shadow of the brilliance of the Stanislaus period. Despite its population having dwindled to a third within a few years, musical life still throve, thanks partly to the tastes of Prussian officials. One of them was E.T.A. Hoffmann, who organized a Music Club (a model for many future Polish Musical Societies) and sponsored concerts at which Beethoven's symphonies were performed for the first time in Poland (1805). Music-printing flourished, and Bogusławski's theatre was still carrying on, drawing heavily on a repertoire of opera and ballet and, apart from a number of Polish operas, in 1802 staging Mozart's *The Magic Flute* in a Polish translation. The development was most marked, however, on the teaching front: in 1811 a drama school with a department of music was opened at Bogusławski's theatre, and ten years later came the establishment of the Conservatoire, where Chopin was to study in 1826—29. The manufacture and sale of musical instruments, the weekly Tygodnik Muzyczny founded in 1820, public concerts and soirées in the salons of the aristocracy, were further features of the rich fabric of music in Warsaw in the first decades of the 19th century, which was only swept away in the tide of reprisals that followed the rising of 1830.

Next to opera, the greatest popularity was enjoyed by piano music. Of the pre-Romantic composers the most successful was Michał Kleofas Ogiński (1765—1833), the scion of a princely family politically active during the reign of Stanislaus Augustus, who wrote many polonaises for piano as well as songs and operas. Another whose piano pieces are of considerable merit was Maria Szymanowska (1789—1831), a talented composer and concert pianist who made a European reputation and is additionally noteworthy for clearly intimating the sources which Chopin was to tap, her works including polonaises, nocturnes, études and mazurkas which anticipate him in more respects than the similarity of names and forms. Piano music was also written by Franciszek Lessel (notably *Piano Concerto in C major*), Józef Elsner, Karol Kurpiński, Józef Deszczyński, Franciszek Mirecki, Feliks Ostrowski, and others. Their compositions, often of very respectable artistic quality, hovered between the classical and the early Romantic *brillant* veins and ploughed the soil in which Chopin's distinctive style was nurtured.

A sizable library could be amassed from the vast amount of material written about Frédéric Chopin (1810—49), Poland's greatest composer of the Romantic period and one of the greatest in the history of music. Both his opus and his life are full of fascinating issues, the discussion of which is beyond the scope of

33

this book. Let us therefore recapitulate only the most important facts. He was born in Żelazowa Wola near Warsaw, the son of Mikołaj Chopin, a Polonized Frenchman, married to a Polish girl. His childhood and adolescence were spent in Warsaw, and at a very early age he began to display an exceptional musical talent, first appearing in public as an eight-year-old boy and becoming the favourite of Warsaw's aristocratic salons. His first piano teacher was Wojciech Żywny who also noted down his first composing efforts. In 1826—29, he studied under Józef Elsner at the Warsaw Conservatoire, winning growing acknowledgement of his gifts as pianist and composer. In 1829, he made his début in Vienna; encouraged by his success there, he set out again the following year, bent on making his name. His itinerary led to Paris, via Wrocław, Vienna and Munich, where he gave concerts. The outbreak and defeat of the 1830 Rising made his return to Poland impossible. Though never active in politics, he belonged to the generation which was most deeply involved in the insurrectionary movement and consequently the target of the severest reprisals. In any case the decline in social and cultural life which followed the suppression of the rising meant there was no place in Warsaw for an artist of Chopin's calibre; even the Conservatoire had been closed by the Tsarist authorities. Chopin settled, therefore, in Paris joining the numerous and colourful group of distinguished patriots, scholars and artists in exile.

When he left Poland, Chopin was already, despite his years, a mature creative artist — with both his piano concertos, a number of études and a great many minor works behind him. Robert Schumann's historic exclamation, *Hut' ab, ihr Herrn, ein Genie!*, on hearing the

Variations on a Theme from Mozart's Don Giovanni (op. 2) in late 1831 was no idle complement. Indeed, Chopin became one of the central figures of the artistic life of Paris almost from the moment of his arrival. A close friend of Liszt, Bellini, Mendelssohn, Berlioz and many other famous musicians, he also made an instant hit with Paris audiences and critics, giving numerous concerts, composing and teaching intensively. Piano lessons were, in fact, his main means of support. After an initial affair with the beautiful Delfina Potocka, he met the famous and eccentric novelist George Sand in 1836, a liaison that continued for more than ten years and gave him the entrée to the circles in which moved such artists as Balzac and Delacroix.

These artistic and aristocratic connections made Chopin as lionized in the Polish emigré world as the great poet Adam Mickiewicz. Although his was the supra-national language of music, far from yielding to the temptation of pulling up his Polish roots, he invariably emphasized them, and the brilliance of his music, so steeped in folk rhythms and melodies, resoundingly asserted that Poland, though wiped off the map, lived on in the hearts of millions and that her spirit could never be crushed. Without engaging in any specific political activity, Chopin thus grew into one of the most effective propagators of the Polish cause. For Schumann the national strains in his music were "guns hidden in flowers". Awareness of the political punch of his haunting but seemingly rarefied music led to attempts by the occupying powers to buy his loyalty with the offer of such titles as *premier pianiste de Sa Majesté l'Empereur de Russie*. Chopin, however, was not to be wooed back by such lures. He made several journeys to Germany, visited Britain — but Paris remained his base. Meanwhile he was being increasingly limited as both concert performer and composer by failing health, and in the autumn of 1849 the consumption that had been eating away his organism finally, despite the devoted care of many friends, took its toll.

Mickiewicz and other Paris friends had, like Elsner before them in Warsaw, tried to persuade Chopin to go in for opera, then generally regarded as the loftiest kind of music, beside which piano compositions were merely a drawing-room entertainment. Chopin would have none of this. True he wrote some chamber works and a number of songs, but they were quite marginal to an opus comprising over 200 items of various size. It was this resistance to the fashions and judgments of his times, the deliberate limitation of his means of expression to the piano — from which he was able, however, to wrest an incredible wealth of musical feeling — that made and make Chopin a unique phenomenon in the history of music.

Three periods have been distinguished in Chopin's work: youthful, up to his departure from Poland, romantic, up to 1839, and classical, the last ten years of his life. The designations are entirely conventional and mean nothing as regards evolution of style which was so smooth that any such classification is bound to be an over-simplifaction. Its only point, therefore, is to indicate the aspects which came uppermost at the different stages of his life.

Thus the predominant feature of the first period are the influences of his Polish predecessors, though enriched by contact with Haydn and Mozart, Hummel, Weber, Field and other forerunners of romantic piano music. These ties remained stamped on the whole of his opus, but it is in these earliest works that the legacy of Ogiński, Lessel, Ostrowski and Szymanowska is most obvious, and the overcoming of the *brillant* style by giving piano virtuosity a significance that goes beyond a mere display of technical mastery. The second period saw the Chopin style in full flower, manifested in the developed forms of one-movement ballads, nocturnes and, in particular, mazurkas which are expressive miniatures with a refinedly simple outward piano form. The harmonic range was extended and amplified, the personal character of the expression intensified. In the third period, Chopin arrived at a synthesis of what he had already developed with the classical sonata and extended one-movement forms: the polonaise, for example, became a sort of poem of complex construction. The third period brought into maximum concentration the features of the Chopin style which Liszt, Wagner, Debussy, Scriabin and Szymanowski were later inspired to build on.

In each of these three periods, Chopin broke new or even revolutionary ground in his mining of the colour and expression potentialities of the piano, his attitude towards Polish folk music and transmutation of its harmonics and rhythmics, and his treatment of form, liberated from classicist fetters, but still logical and coherent. It is a remarkable attribute of his music that, revolutionary as it was, it met with such a vivid and immediate response among his contemporaries. Another is that, while it was a supreme example of a national style and spoke of matters dearest to his fellow-countrymen of the first half of the 19th century, it stirred, as it still does, the hearts of people all over the world, however remote from things Polish.

The only Polish composer of the 19th century whom Chopin's greatness did not thoroughly overshadow in the general consciousness of the Polish public was Stanisław Moniuszko, probably because he appealed to the same national feelings. Moniuszko's achievement, however, was to do so with songs and operas which employed the words of the mother tongue which in his day was being ruthlessly eradicated by the partitioning powers from education and from public life. Moniuszko thus took Chopin's mantle and performed in the second half of the 19th century the same public role as Chopin had in the first. Musically, however, there were many differences between them since Moniuszko was heir to operatic traditions as created by Elsner and Kurpiński.

Józef Elsner (1769—1854), composer and conductor, associated with Bogusławski's theatre, founder and principal of Poland's first conservatoire (1821) was, in addition to being Chopin's tutor, a man who rendered great services to Polish music. One of Warsaw's main authorities in his field in the first decades of the 19th century, he was also a prominent freemason, who, though of foreign birth, devoted all his energies to Polish culture. He composed symphonic works, chamber and piano music and, above all, numerous operas in an eclectic style, chiefly historial subject.

Karol Kurpiński (1785—1857), also connected with Bogusławski's theatre and an equally conspicuous figure in Poland's music life (director of the Warsaw Opera in the years 1824—40), was more original as a composer. Of his rich and diversified opus, it was the operas which enjoyed the greatest popularity. Some of them like *Pałac Lucypera* (Lucifer's Palace), *Szarlatan* (The Charlatan), and *Zabobon czyli nowe krakowiaki* (Superstition or the New Cracovians) are now enjoying modernized revivals. Kurpiński was a self-taught composer but acquired considerable expertise and created a musical style of his own which combined the typical features of Rossini with the national accents of Polish folk rhythms and melodies. His interest in folk music found another outlet in his articles for the weekly Tygodnik Muzyczny which he had founded in 1820 and which also bore witness to a nascent interest in Polish music of the past centuries.

There were many other composers of lesser note though just as well known in their day; Franciszek Mirecki (1791—1862), Tomasz Nidecki (1807—52), Józef Damse (1788—1852), etc. An exceptional figure, worth recalling, was Prince Antoni Radziwiłł (1775—1833). Not that he was an isolated case in the Polish aristocracy, many of whom dabbled in music, e.g. the Ogińskis, the Wielhorskis, Wacław Rzewuski, and other members of the music-loving Radziwiłł family. However, Antoni Radziwiłł was genuinely talented. His main work was a setting of Goethe's *Faust*, many years in the writing and completed in 1831. Chopin, who visited the Prince at his country house near Poznań two years earlier, was full of praise. Even Goethe, suspicious and exacting as he was, was very pleased and, at the composer's request, agreed to certain changes and additions to his tragedy. Radziwiłł's work enjoyed great success in Germany in the 19th century.

Stanisław Moniuszko (1819—72) remains a composer of great reputation and popularity in Poland, but practically unknown abroad. This is probably due to his principal aim being to satisfy the musical and spiritual needs of his contemporaries in a country which, subjugated and cut off from the world, was unable to promote its leading composer more widely. Nevertheless, Moniuszko's life and work are wonderfully revealing of Polish mentalities in the late 19th century. He was born into a family of small landowners in what was then eastern Poland and displayed musical gifts from childhood. After studying under the organist August Freyer in Warsaw and Dominik Stefanowicz in Minsk, he attended in 1837—40 the composition class of Carl Rungenhagen, at the Singakademie in Berlin. It was there that he first heard the score of Radziwiłł's *Faust* which Rungenhagen was completing after the composer's death. In 1840, he settled in Vilna where he found a post as organist, conducted an orchestra, organized concerts — and soon became a central figure in its musical world. In the course of tours to St. Petersburg he made the close acquaintance of such distinguished Russian musicians as Glinka, Dargomyzhski, Cui and Serov and on similar visits to Warsaw he found friends among progressive writers and music critics (Józef Sikorski). During his 18 years in Vilna, Moniuszko composed prolifically, the many works he wrote there including the first version of his most famous opera, *Halka,* the orchestral overture *Bajka* — highly praised by the critics in St. Petersburg — and a number of operettas, vaudevilles and songs. In 1858, a new version of *Halka* was produced at the Wielki (Grand) Theatre in Warsaw. Its immense success led to an invitation to assume the management of the opera section in the Grand Theatre. He accepted, moved to Warsaw and from then on was plunged into the heart of the arts world, occupying himself with opera composition and teaching at the Warsaw Conservatoire, which had been revived in 1861 through the efforts of Apolinary Kątski. In spite of the great success of each new work with the Polish public, he was unable to arouse any interest either in Paris or in Germany which he visited especially for this purpose. Although *Halka* was produced in Prague, Moscow and St. Petersburg during his lifetime, the indifference, invariably shown to him by the European „grand monde", was not to be overcome. In those days, the worst possible thing that could happen to a talented artist was to be born in Poland.

Moniuszko's chief achievement was the creation of a national opera style; his role was similar to that of Glinka in Russia and Smetana in Bohemia. He composed serious and comic operas, operettas and vaudevilles, social in subject, national in character, avoiding the fantastic and historical themes, so typical of Romanticism. Nor was he interested in the contemporary experiments with musical drama, confining himself to traditional opera forms. In harmony, too, he remained conventional and made no attempt even to approach the trail blazed by Chopin. Nor was Polish folklore tapped as liberally. On the other hand, he drew profusely on the wealth of Polish national dances to produce the most superb artistic versions of the polonaise and the mazurka. The distinctive feature of his temperament was, for all its casting in the romantic mould, a strong social and patriotic instinct which ruled out the practice of „art for art's sake" and made him devote all his gifts to the service of society and its needs.

The value of Moniuszko's work lay primarily in the musical formulation of the idea of Polishness: viewed in the context of the plight of a nation fighting to preserve their threatened identity and looking to art, above all, for the reaffirmation of their spiritual independence, it stands out enhanced. In this respect, Moniuszko resembles the great Polish painter, Jan Matejko

(1838—93), who similarly indifferent to contemporary currents in European art, created huge historical tableaux, recalling the landmarks of Poland's past and giving arresting artistic form to its people, events and ideas. Matejko, however, lived in the relatively liberal Austrian-ruled part of Poland, whereas Moniuszko was muzzled by the constraints of the Tsarist censorship which stamped down on any overt manifestation of patriotism. As a result the theatre of that time, Moniuszko's operas and Warsaw audiences were pervaded by a battle of wits the censor waged by means of various allusions, hidden meanings and symbols. Apart from *Halka*, with its abundance of forceful social overtones, a very conspicuous role in keeping up the patriotic spirit in society was played by the excellent comic opera *Straszny Dwór* (The Haunted Manor), in many ways the finest of his works. The Polish ethos was also perfectly caught in other comic operas, such as *Hrabina* (The Countess) and *Verbum nobile*.

Quantitatively, however, pride of place in Moniuszko's work belongs to his songs, written in response to a wide community need. Since they were intended for performance by amateurs, he avoided intricate forms and excessive technical difficulties. All the same, his extraordinary melodic inventiveness, closely connected with folk songs, and his subtle sense of the miniature form, make these songs, collected in the twelve volumes of *Śpiewniki domowe* (Home Song-books), bear comparison with Schubert. The solo and choral pieces remained to the end of the 19th century a staple of the music-making so popular in Polish homes and they are still firm favourites. Less widely known are his cantatas, e.g. *Widma* (The Phantoms), *Sonety krymskie* (Crimean Sonnets), *Litanie ostrobramskie* (The Ostra

Brama Litanies), though he himself set great store by them. Moniuszko was no innovator; on the contrary, in many respects he trailed behind the bold march forward of European music. He did so quite deliberately, though not without bitterness, realizing that if he wanted to be of use to his countrymen, he had to forgo higher aspirations and cut his coat according to his audience.

Carrying on down the path signposted by Chopin in the purely musical sense was not possible in the circumstances of Moniuszko's day. Consequently by the time his prolific output had become a tradition for succeeding generations of composers lacking the ability to marry it to the achievements of European music, it degenerated into an epigonism that was not overcome until the beginning of the 20th century.

A separate category of musicians in the 19th century were the virtuosi. Chopin's genius eclipsed the talents of other Polish pianists, but there were many famous violinists, and several of them were also interesting composers. Apart from the aforementioned Feliks Janiewicz, mention is also due to August Duranowski (1770—1834), a pupil of Viotti, who performed with great success in Italy, Germany and France. Paganini used to say that he owed a part of his technical skills to Duranowski.

Reckoned a rival to Paganini was Karol Lipiński (1790—1861) ever since a violin tournament in Piacenza in 1818, at which they were ranked equal. A second encounter in 1829 in Warsaw confirmed this reputation. For a long time he was considered the greatest living Polish musician. Chopin was entranced by his playing and Schumann, Berlioz and the young Wagner were full of praise. Lipiński was also a prolific composer, writing virtuoso violin concertos, rondos and concerto polonaises; of particular value are his *Capriccios* for solo violin, published in a number of collections, which astounded his contemporaries with their technical complexities.

Lipiński's successor was Henryk Wieniawski (1835—80), one of the most famous virtuosi of the 19th century. He studied in Paris under Lambert Massart and began to give concerts at the age of 13, appearing together with his brother Józef, a distinguished pianist. In 1860, he became court soloist in St. Petersburg where he also taught at the Conservatoire. Wieniawski made concert tours all over Europe and in the United States (with Anton Rubinstein and Pauline Lucca). He composed virtuoso violin works, distinguished for their elegance of form. Some of them, e.g. *Concerto in F-Sharp Minor* (op. 14), *Concerto in D Minor* (op. 22), *Concert Fantasia on Themes from Gounod's "Faust"* (op. 20), *Polonaise in A Major* for violin and orchestra (op. 21), have become standard pieces for violin virtuosi. To commemorate this greatest of Polish violinists, a Henryk Wieniawski International Violin Competition was inaugurated in Poland in 1935 and is held every five years (1935, 1952, 1957, 1962, 1967, 1972).

From among the host of violinists of this period, mention should also be made of Apolinary Kątski (1825—79), a pupil of Paganini, who rendered great services to musical culture, mainly by re-opening the Conservatoire in Warsaw (1861), closed down by the Russian authorities after the 1830 Rising. A name was also made by Nikodem Biernacki (1826—92), for several years court violinist in Stockholm, and by Izydor Lotto (c. 1840—1936), a pupil of Massart, who, like Wieniawski, first appeared in public as a boy. Among pianists, the greatest international acclaim was won by Józef Wieniawski (1837—1912), active chiefly in Brussels, Karol Tausig (1841—71), a pupil of Liszt, author of numerous virtuoso transcriptions and arrangements, and Juliusz Zarębski (1854—85), another pupil of Liszt, and also a composer of exceptionally original gifts, whose development was cut short by an early death.

In the middle of the 19th century, folk music also began to claim attention. Interest in this age-old, anonymous partner of the artist had been born during the Enlightenment. It grew greatly in the era of Romanticism, when it began to bear its first fruits in the form of song collections, articles and treatises. These were still amateur endeavours; in the same way the creative use Chopin and other composers made of folk music was a purely intuitive matter, with no thorough knowledge of the field behind it.

It was only with the appearance of Oskar Kolberg (1814—90) that Polish ethnography emerged as a science. It was, however, an impressive beginning. Kolberg, a composer by education, a public servant by profession, came of the same background as Chopin. He became interested in folk music more or less accidentally and treated it at first as material for his own compositions. Gradually, however, the number of folk songs noted down by him multiplied and his working methods became more scientific. After the publication of his first collection (1842), Kolberg abandoned the practice, common at that time, of elaborating on the original melodies, adding piano accompaniment, etc. The romantic enchantment with folk music and poetry gave way to the meticulous approach of a scholar bent on systematization and comparative study. Kolberg's concerns soon widened and their range is indicated by the title of his monumental work: *Lud, jego zwyczaje, spo-sób życia, mowa, podania, przysłowia, obrzędy, gusła, zabawy, pieśni, muzyka i tańce* (The People, Its Customs, Way of Life, Speech, Legends, Proverbs, Rites, Runes, Entertainments, Songs, Music and Dances). This multi-volume publication began to appear in 1865 and, together with the volumes published after the author's death, it contains nearly 20,000 folk melodies from various regions of Poland as well as material from other fields of vernacular culture. Kolberg's life work had no precedent in the world in its dimensions and compass, and it became the foundation of Polish musical ethnography. His collections, still being enlarged, saved the riches of Polish folk culture from oblivion and have been a continuing inspiration to our artists down to the present day. For example, a considerable part of the repertoire of the famous "Mazowsze" and "Śląsk" ensembles is drawn from this source.

The revival noticeable in the second half of the 19th century in certain areas of Polish musical culture did not, unfortunately, characterize it as a whole. The hard times made its natural development very slow, and music life fell behind that of other countries of Europe. The situation in the Austrian-ruled part of the country, where the centres of arts and learning were Cracow and Lvov, was relatively the most favourable. The internal policy of the Habsburg monarchy was fairly liberal thanks to which their Polish dominions also obtained a certain degree of autonomy. The Universities of Cracow and Lvov and the Academy of Learning founded in Cracow in 1871, radiated an influence all over Poland. In the Prussian and Russian zones, on the other hand, remorseless campaigns were mounted to de-nationalize the Poles, the youth above all. After the

January Rising, there was a wave of reprisals against all those suspected of contacts with the insurgents and any spontaneous manifestations of patriotism were stifled. At the same time, the development of industry, especially in Warsaw and Łódź, led to a rapid growth of the urban proletariat; and a nascent working-class movement, also fiercely persecuted by the partitioning powers, came into being.

No wonder, therefore that in such circumstances music life in Poland slackened considerably. Music had a raison d'être only in so far as it could be an oblique political demonstration aimed at reinforcing the sense of national identity and preserving the Polish language. Consequently the interests of the community were in the second half of the 19th century captured chiefly by songs. The basic repertoire, created by Stanisław Moniuszko, was now amplified by subsequent generations of composers.

A particularly important role was also played by the rapidly growing number of choral societies. By the end of the 19th century, a network of amateur clubs cultivating Polish music had spread all over Poland. Higher artistic aspirations were embraced by the Warsaw Music Society, founded in 1870, and the Galicia Music Society, founded in Lvov in 1858. Journals were another vehicle of the struggle for Polish culture: in 1857, Józef Sikorski, Moniuszko's friend and callaborator, started the weekly Ruch Muzyczny; in 1877, Echo Muzyczne i Teatralne, edited by Jan Kleczyński, began to appear. Interest in old Polish music was revived, the first studies of Chopin's work were published, the seeds of Polish musicology were sown.

Composing, however, suffered from the absence of a permanent symphony orchestra and the marked hostility of the management of the opera houses in Warsaw and Lvov to Polish works. Composers, therefore, confined themselves for the most part to smaller pieces which had a greater chance of public performance and the more gifted artists sought careers abroad. There were quite a number of these. The famous violinists and pianists already mentioned were joined at the end of the 19th century by new names of the violinist Stanisław Barcewicz (1858—1929), the pianist Aleksander Michałowski (1851—1938) and the legendary Ignacy Paderewski (1860—1941) who, ever since his Vienna début in 1887, remained a star of the first magnitude for many years. Towards the end of the 19th century, there also appeared in Poland a whole galaxy of singers who made international reputations and became part of the history of vocal art. Suffice it to mention Władysław Mierzwiński, Mieczysław Kamiński, Jan and Edward Reszke, Aleksander Bandrowski or Marcelina Sembrich-Kochańska.

For reasons already explained, the composers who succeeder Stanisław Moniuszko cannot compete with their German, Russian, French or Italian contemporaries. At a time when European music was enjoying one of its heydays, Polish music was stricken by the hardest period of its history.

The best known Polish composer at that time was Władysław Żeleński (1837—1921), author of the operas *Konrad Wallenrod, Goplana, Stara Baśń* (An Old Tale), numerous songs, piano and chamber music, and several symphonic works, among which the overture *W Tatrach* (In the Tatra Mountains) enjoyed the greatest popularity. Żeleński's style, though it had certain individual traits, followed in the footsteps of German Romanticism, as represented by Mendelssohn, Schumann and Brahms. The other composer of note was Zygmunt

Noskowski (1846—1909), a pupil of Moniuszko, who showed perhaps the greatest interest in the contemporary currents in European music. Of greatest importance in his profuse output were the symphonic works, none too common in the Polish music of this period. His concert overture *Morskie Oko* (op. 19) and *Step* (The Steppe) (op. 66), the first symphonic poem in Polish music composed in 1896, became particularly popular. Noskowski was also for many years a professor of composition at the Warsaw Conservatoire, and trained almost a whole generation of composers, the ones who were to revive Polish music in the 20th century.

Among composers contemporary to Żeleński and Noskowski, mention is due also to Adam Münchheimer and Ludwik Grossmann (operas), Jan Gall and Eugeniusz Pankiewicz (songs), and Aleksander Zarzycki, Antoni Stolpe and Roman Statkowski (piano music).

RECORDINGS BY "POLSKIE NAGRANIA—MUZA" OF 19th-CENTURY POLISH MUSIC (selection)

Maciej Kamieński: *Tradycja dowcipem załatwiona* (Tradition Settled by Wit), opera
The Warsaw Chamber Opera under the direction of Stefan Sutkowski. XL 0617

Józef Elsner: *Król Łokietek albo Wiśliczanki* (King Ladislaus the Short or the Girls from Wiślicz), opera in two acts
Soloists, Choir of the National Philharmonic, Orchestra of the Warsaw Chamber Opera, conducted by Jerzy Dobrzański. XL 0542

Polish Pre-Romantic Piano Music (Michał Kleofas Ogiński, Feliks Janiewicz, Franciszek Lessel, Maria Szymanowska)
Regina Smendzianka, piano. XL 0355

Early Polish Piano Music (Stanisław Moniuszko, Maria Szymanowska, Karol Kurpiński, Maciej Kamieński, Wojciech Żywny)
Lidia Kozubek, piano. XL 0559

Franciszek Lessel: *Piano Concerto in C Major*
Zbigniew Drzewiecki (piano), the National Philharmonic Orchestra, conducted by Stanisław Wisłocki. XL 0176

Frédéric Chopin: Complete Works, played by Polish artists. 25 records

Frédéric Chopin: *Piano Concerto in F Minor*
Witold Małcużyński (piano), the National Philharmonic Orchestra, conducted by Witold Rowicki. XL 0048

Frédéric Chopin: *Piano Concerto in E Minor*
Martha Argerich (piano), the National Philharmonic Orchestra, conducted by Witold Rowicki. XL 0265

Frédéric Chopin: Piano Works
Garrick Ohlsson, piano. XL 0689

Frédéric Chopin: Piano Works
Jeffrey Swann, piano. XL 0685, XL 0686

Karol Lipiński: *Violin Concerto in D Major*
Igor Iwanow (violin), the National Philharmonic Orchestra, conducted by Stanisław Wisłocki, XL 0176

Stanisław Moniuszko: *Songs from the Home Song-books* (selection)
Andrzej Hiolski (baritone), Sergiusz Nadgryzowski (piano). XL 0545

Stanisław Moniuszko: *Songs from the Home Song-books* (selection)
Halina Szymulska (soprano), Jerzy Lefeld (piano). XL 0619

Stanisław Moniuszko: *1st String Quartet*. Piano Works
String quartet: Magdalena Rezler, Maria Słubicka, Marek Marczyk, Jerzy Andrzejczak, Regina Smendzianka (piano). XL 0546

Stanisław Moniuszko: *Halka,* opera in four acts
Soloists, Polish Radio Grand Symphony Orchestra, Choir of the Polish Radio in Cracow, conducted by Jerzy Semkow. XL 0872—4

Stanisław Moniuszko: *Verbum nobile,* opera in one act
Soloists, Choir and Orchestra of the Stanisław Moniuszko Opera in Poznań, conducted by Robert Satanowski. XL 0526—7

Juliusz Zarębski: *Piano Quintet in G Minor*
The Warsaw Quintet. XL 0178

Juliusz Zarębski: Piano Works
Ryszard Bakst, piano. XL 0255

Henryk Wieniawski: *Violin Concerto No. 2 in D Minor*
Wanda Wiłkomirska (violin), the National Philharmonic Orchestra, conducted by Witold Rowicki. XL 0113

Władysław Żeleński: *W Tatrach* (In the Tatra Mountains), overture
The National Philharmonic Orchestra, conducted by Witold Rowicki. XL 0259

Zygmunt Noskowski: *Step* (The Steppe), symphonic poem; *Szki-ce węglem* (Crayon Sketches), overture; *Elegiac Polonaise; Mor-skie Oko,* overture

The National Philharmonic Orchestra, conducted by Witold Rowicki. XL 0259

III. CATCHING UP WITH EUROPE — FIRST ATTEMPT

*On the Threshold of the 20th Century; Ignacy Pa-
derewski; Birth of the Warsaw Philharmonic; the
"Young Poland in Music" Group; Mieczysław Karłowicz; Karol Szymanowski — his Work and Significance; Music in Reborn Poland; To Paris, for Education; Operas, Philharmonics, International Competitions and Festivals*

The 20th century found Poland in a sorry state. In
the Prussian zone the Polish population was struggling
against an increasingly vicious Germanization drive led
by the "Hakate" nationalist organization which was
bent on stamping out all things Polish and clearing
the way to complete German settlement. In the Austrian-ruled part of the country — the most liberal —
general social development was checked by economic
backwardness and rural over-population. In the Rus-
sian-held territories, on the other hand, the first years
of the 20th century saw substantial changes in the wake
of the Russo-Japanese war and the revolution of
1905, above all an extension of political freedoms and
relaxation of the cultural constraints. Meanwhile the
brewing European conflicts held out new hopes, the
prospect of war between Poland's hitherto allied ene-
mies seeming to offer a real chance of regaining independence, either, depending on political orientation,
with the help of Russia or Austria, or by means of
a revolution. In fact events took yet another course.

Poland's cultural life in these years was concentrated in Warsaw, Cracow and Lvov. In the course of World War I, the lead was taken by Warsaw which has since been the political and intellectual centre of the country. Music life, however, still languished. The nation was impoverished and preoccupied with social and political affairs. There were no institutions capable of piloting it back on to the map, nor artists of sufficient stature. The heights scaled by European music through the creative talents of Mahler, Debussy, Strauss, Scriabin — and, shortly thereafter, Schönberg, Stravinsky and the whole generation of modernists — seemed altogether beyond our reach.

The most famous Polish musician of this period was the pianist, Ignacy Paderewski (1860—1941), who achieved immense success all over the world, especially in the United States. He was also a composer, the author of *Piano Concerto in A Minor, Polish Fantasia* for piano and orchestra, *Symphony in B minor,* the opera *Manru,* and a number of other works. All the same, Saint-Saëns' frequently quoted opinion that Paderewski was a "genius who also happens to play the piano" seems somewhat exaggerated. Though certainly a gifted composer, he did not exert a major influence on the evolution of Polish music, if only because he was mainly active outside Poland. His international celebrity was turned to different account: during World War I, he launched an extensive campaign in the United States for Polish independence. He was also briefly Premier and Foreign Minister in the first Polish government after independence was recovered in 1918.

Another great artist who could only find opportunities to develop outside Poland was the famous harpsichordist Wanda Landowska (1879—1959), a pupil of

Aleksander Michałowski. The pianist and composer Henryk Melcer (1869—1928) was similarly forced to spend a great part of his life abroad, and Zygmunt Stojowski (1870—1946), after his early European success as pianist and composer, left for the United States in 1906 to settle for good. Others who lived abroad for prolonged periods of time were Feliks Nowowiejski (1877—1946), Witold Maliszewski (1873—1939) and Eugeniusz Morawski (1876—1948). In Poland Żeleński and Noskowski continued to be the main influences. They were joined on the scene by Roman Statkowski (1859—1925), Stanisław Niewiadomski (1859—1936), and many other composers who were unable however to lift music out of its general stagnation. But now a new generation, educated at the Warsaw Conservatoire under Zygmunt Noskowski, was approaching maturity and was soon to usher in a great revival.

The first spur came from the opening of the Warsaw Philharmonic in 1901 which made the dreams of several generations of composers for that most important of all instruments — a symphony orchestra — a reality. The programme of the inaugural concert on 5 November, enhanced by the appearance of Ignacy Paderewski, contained works by Chopin, Moniuszko, Żeleński, Noskowski, Stojowski and Paderewski. The orchestra was, at first, largely composed of foreigners but also included some young Polish musicians whose names were soon to become well known, notably Grzegorz Fitelberg, Paweł Kochański and Henryk Opieński. It was put in the charge of a young composer and conductor, Emil Młynarski (1870—1935), who soon became one of Poland's best known concert-platform figures, particularly in Britain and the United States, and later became manager of the Grand Theatre (Warsaw's opera house). The administrative and financial structure of the Warsaw Philharmonic was, however, rather complex, and from the start it had to labour under difficulties which seriously threatened its survival on more than one occasion. What is more, the Warsaw public so long without such a musical institution, was not accustomed to regular concert-going, and the management of the Philharmonic had to bend over backwards to lure them by booking the most famous artists of the day. In terms of the great virtuosi and conductors who appeared at the beginning of the century, these were dazzling seasons. Warsaw was suddenly plunged into a concert life similar to that of the great capitals of Europe. This was, however, not an unmixed blessing. In its endeavours to woo audiences, the Philharmonic let down the hopes of young composers who had a very hard time gaining admittance to the country's one permanent concert stage and even if they did, found themselves up against the increasing hostility of the conservatives.

The young composers in question were four pupils of Zygmunt Noskowski, linked by personal ties of friendship and common hopes of reviving Polish music through its modernization and Europeanization: Grzegorz Fitelberg, Ludomir Różycki, Apolinary Szeluto and Karol Szymanowski. They were later joined by the somewhat older Mieczysław Karłowicz. This group called itself "Young Poland in Music" to match a movement that had sprung up at the end of the 19th century in the fine arts and literature. They were determined to break with the imitativeness of the post-Moniuszko period by taking their bearings from the contemporary European avant-garde as symbolized by Richard Strauss, which they saw as the only way of rescuing our music from its provincialism and giving it a modern and national character. In 1905, with the financial aid of Prince Władysław Lubomirski, they set up "The Young Polish Composers' Publishing Company", and in 1906 organized the first joint concert of their works at the Warsaw Philharmonic. Their appearance was received with enthusiasm, but an acute conflict soon arose between the conservative public and critics and the "Young Poland" composers who were accused of cosmopolitanism, aping German models and betraying national traditions. The future was to prove these charges absurd and that a group of truly remarkable figures had arrived who were to set the development of Polish music on a new course.

The eldest of them was Mieczysław Karłowicz (1876—1909), a lover of the mountains who was killed by an avalanche in the Tatras. After studying the violin under Stanisław Barcewicz and composition under Zygmunt Noskowski, he left for Berlin to continue his training as a violinist under Joseph Joachim but instead switched to composition under Heinrich Urban. The thorough knowledge of contemporary music acquired there directed his interest chiefly to the symphonic poem which became his main genre. Karłowicz's career, though cut so brutally short by his fatal accident, nevertheless brought a number of works of great value and of considerable importance to Polish music. Among his youthful compositions, the best are the beautiful *Violin Concerto in A Major,* written for Stanisław Barcewicz, and the *Serenade* for string orchestra, both of which are close to Tchaikovsky. His later, deeply felt symphonic poems — *Powracające fale* (Recurring Waves), *Odwieczne pieśni* (Immemorial Songs), *Rapsodia litewska* (Lithuanian Rhapsody), *Stanisław i Anna Oświęcimowie* (Stanisław and Anna

Oświęcim), *Smutna opowieść* (A Sad Tale) and the un-finished *Epizod na maskaradzie* (Episode at a Masked Ball) — brought Polish symphonic music up to a European standard and sprang from an individual interpretation of the achievements of late-Romantic German composers.

The "Young Poland" group disintegrated fairly quickly. Karłowicz died; the others were parted by differing interests, dispositions and abilities. Grzegorz Fitelberg (1879—1953), who had started out with a number of interesting orchestral works written in the years 1901—8, soon concentrated exclusively on conducting and in this capacity energetically championed the new Polish music, especially Karłowicz and Szymanowski. It was he who had conducted that historic first concert of the "Young Poland" group in 1906, and two years later became the conductor of the Warsaw Philharmonic. Next to Emil Młynarski, he was the foremost Polish conductor of the day and of the period between the two World Wars, rendering immense services to Polish music and its propagation outside Poland.

Apolinary Szeluto (1884—1966) devoted himself to piano and legal studies. His vast range of interests and prodigious powers of invention made him compose very fast and in every vein, but he squandered his gifts, failed to develop an original style of his own and played no role in the history of Polish music.

Ludomir Różycki (1884—1953) was originally drawn to symphonic music, which constituted the link with Karłowicz and Szymanowski, and composed a number of symphonic poems — *Stańczyk, Anhelli, Mona Lisa* — modelled, particularly in their instrumentation, on Richard Strauss. Compared with the highly personal note struck by Karłowicz's poems, they are more illustrative in character and depend for their effect on the dazzle of the sound design. Early in his career, however, Różycki turned to stage music and became popular as the composer of the operas *Bolesław Śmiały* (Boleslaus the Bold), *Eros i Psyche, Casanova,* and *Beatrix Cenci,* and the ballets *Pan Twardowski* and *Apollo i dziewczyna* (Apollo and the Girl). His exemplars were Wagner and Puccini, and the success he enjoyed abroad as well as in Poland may have been partly due to his indifference to contemporary avantgarde experiments and adherence to the beaten track of the late-Romantic style.

The only one of the entire "Young Poland" group to remain true to its original ideals was Karol Szymanowski (1882—1937), the greatest figure in Polish music after Chopin and its main ideologue in the years preceding World War I and in the inter-war period. Born into a family of small landowners in the Ukraine, he studied piano under Gustaw Neuhaus and composition under Zygmunt Noskowski though only on a private, part-time basis, and was in fact an auto-didact, gifted with an exceptional natural grasp and insight. Bound from his youth by close friendship with the pianist Artur Rubinstein, the violinist Paweł Kochański, and the conductor Grzegorz Fitelberg, he soon became the leading light of the younger Polish composers.

Students of Szymanowski's work distinguish three periods: pre-1914, World War I, and post-independence. The coincidence with historical dates is no more than that, the only connexion being the influence of external events on his personal fortunes and *eo ipso facto* on his work. Common to all three was an ambition to reach the forefront of European music; the differences lay in the way he pursued this goal and the clarity with which he saw where he was heading.

In the first period, Szymanowski hammered out the technical aspects of his craft, beginning with piano miniatures and songs and gradually moving on to more elaborate forms. His style was still very much of a mixture — Chopin, Brahms, Scriabin, Reger and Strauss are all variously to be heard in *Piano Preludes* (op. 1), *Piano Variations in B flat Minor, Concert Overture*, even in best works of this period: the *2nd Piano Sonata, 2nd Symphony* and the one-act opera *Hagith*. Cruelly aware that Polish music had driven itself into a dead end, he turned to foreign sources, but tapped them in no slavish manner. Two things gave him a creatively Polish identity: the influence of the young writers striving to create a modern style with a specifically national stamp, but in the mould of European tastes, and a worship of Chopin. For Szymanowski, Chopin's music was a living tradition which he plumbed at first intuitively, but with increasing sophistication, in marked contrast to the parochial rehash made of it by the post-Moniuszko generation. Szymanowski himself kept fairly continually on the move: frequent visits to Berlin and Leipzig, a longer stay in Vienna, several journeys to Italy and North Africa. These travels drew his attention to the culture of the East and the South; at the same time, closer contact with the music of Debussy and Ravel added to his palette new values that were to be fully revealed in the second period.

Szymanowski spent World War I in the Ukraine, partly at his family home, partly in Kiev; he also visited Moscow and St. Petersburg to hear his works performed. But his chief occupation was composing. The outstanding effort was the *3rd Symphony* called *Pieśń o nocy* (Song of the Night) for high voice, choir and large orchestra, a setting of a 13th-century Arabian poem, the most elaborate orchestral score in Polish music of this date (1914—16). Its feeling of ecstasy and finely-wrought sound colour are an attempt to translate into music the emotions engendered on encountering the culture of the Middle East. It also bears witness to a thorough knowledge of modern composing techniques and in more than one respect — especially in harmony — is of a precursory character. The same Eastern interests gave birth to three cycles of songs for voice and piano, later arranged for voice and orchestra: *Pieśni miłosne Hafiza* (The Love Songs of Hafiz), *Pieśni księżniczki z baśni* (Songs of a Fairy-tale Princess) and *Pieśni muezina szalonego* (Songs of the Mad Muezzin). An additional source of inspiration were the great vocal gifts of his sister, Stanisława Korwin-Szymanowska, a peerless performer of his works. In the same way his long friendship with the famous violinist Paweł Kochański yielded a number of violin works. In this second period, Szymanowski collaborated with him on the composition of, among others, the *1st Violin Concerto* and a set of three poems for violin and piano, *Mity* (Myths). Like two cycles of piano pieces, *Metopy* (Metopes) and *Maski* (Masks), both works represent a response to the harmonious beauty of the South. His travels in Italy, Sicily and Africa and sampling of the riches of ancient and Oriental culture and early Christian art also bore fruit in the opera *Król Roger* (King Roger), with a libretto by Jarosław Iwaszkiewicz, a distinguished Polish writer and one of Szymanowski's closest friends. As a result of historical circumstances, it was long in the writing (1918—24) and by the time it was completed new impulses had already propelled his interests elsewhere.

In 1919, with Poland again an independent state, Szymanowski settled in Warsaw, his Ukrainian birthplace being on the other side of the Curzon Line. By now he was unquestionably Poland's best composer, a fact, however, that was lost on all but a small group and brought painfully home to him by the very first concert of his works. In a letter to the musicologist Zdzisław Jachimecki, his friend and first biographer, he wrote:

I again discovered the same thing that forced me once before to leave Warsaw seven years ago; that between me and the Polish public (or the Warsaw public, at any rate) there is no real contact whatsoever, that I am a perfect stranger to them, and incomprehensible... The provincialism prevailing here simply cannot stomach the European flavour of my art. I stick in their throat because I make them look silly... The concert took place in the hall of the Conservatoire which has 550—600 seats. Despite the names of Paweł Kochański... and my sister being on the bill, it was not sold out. Which means that in the whole of Warsaw 600 people couldn't be found with an interest in what I have been doing for the past 5 years!... The first opportunity I have I will once more leave Warsaw for the West or the South (Italy).

Nevertheless this discouraging atmosphere did not drive Szymanowski out of Poland, though in subsequent years he made several trips abroad which — with the help of Artur Rubinstein and Paweł Kochański — introduced him to the international musical world. Joint concerts in London, Paris and the United States, contacts with Stravinsky and Diaghilev, festivals of the International Society for Contemporary Music (SIMC), all helped eventually to bring him recognition in Poland as well.

In 1927, Szymanowski was appointed Rector of the

Warsaw Conservatoire and held this post — with a one year interval — until 1932. The absence was due to his health: in 1929 it was found that he was suffering from tuberculosis. From then on it was to cast a growing shadow over Szymanowski's life, though even so periods of treatment in nursing homes alternated with ones of increasingly intensive composing. Furthermore a shower of Polish and foreign honours did not ease his financial troubles, and these caused him to return to the concert platform. In 1932, he resigned as head of the Conservatoire over conflicts with conservative music circles, and began a series of tours as a pianist performing his own works. Together with his friends Fitelberg and Kochański, his sister Stanisława, and other musicians, he appeared in many countries, including the USSR. To fill out his repertoire, he composed his *4th Concertante Symphony* for piano and orchestra (1932), a number of minor piano pieces, and drafted the unfinished *Piano Concerto*. He banked heavily on the Paris Opera, for despite the success of *King Roger*, produced in 1926 at the Grand Theatre in Warsaw with Młynarski conducting, and in 1932 in Prague, he realized that to establish himself internationally, he had to make his name in Paris, then the capital of the artistic world. The death of Diaghilev in 1929 had upset what foothold he had, but he succeeded in interesting the Paris Opera for which he composed the ballet *Harnasie* (Highland Robbers), completed in 1931, produced in 1935 in Prague, and in 1936 in Paris, with choreography by Serge Lifar. But its success and his growing international reputation came too late. Tuberculosis finally carried him off in 1937 and World War II that followed shortly obliterated his name from the memory of the European public.

This third period in Szymanowski's oeuvre was the one of the greatest importance in the history of Polish music, not only because it yielded many splendid works but, above all, because it marked the fashioning of a style all his own, which no longer owed anything to foreign influences, and whose folk roots gave it all the characteristics of a national one. The latter was a quality he pursued quite deliberately: when he was writing *Stabat Mater,* he turned for inspiration to old Polish music; with *Harnasie,* it was the music of the highlanders which he discovered at first hand in 1922 in the mountain resort of Zakopane where he became a frequent visitor and settled for good towards the end of his life. At that time Zakopane attracted many leading Polish artists with the beauty of its scenery and the originality of its folk art. What bewitched Szymanowski was its music, utterly unlike that of other regions, and magnificently stimulating in melody, harmony and rhythm. Traces of this fascination can be seen in nearly all the works of the third period: in *Harnasie,* the *4th Symphony,* the numerous mazurkas for piano, the *2nd String Quartet* and the *2nd Violin Concerto.* A second folk influence were the songs of the Kurpie region, which he knew from the published collections. By drawing on these sources he was following the road indicated by Chopin, seeking, like Bartók, to capture the essence of folk music and as the germ knit it into his own creative work. Only very rarely was it transposed bodily (e.g. in *Harnasie*) or adapted (e.g. in *Kurpie Songs*) into solo or choral songs.

Throughout the inter-war period Szymanowski held the centre of Poland's music stage. Not that it was always a kindly spotlight. For the young generation of composers his word was all law, but among older and

conservative-minded musicians he had many antago-
nists. With music life in Poland still struggling to its
feet this gave rise to many conflicts. The resources of
the state were after over a century of servitude stretch-
ed too thin to meet the demand of audiences, so
that the development of such things as publishing or
artistic training staggered through many crises, music
institutions were plagued by financial difficulties and
the powers that be failed to appreciate the educational
and propaganda importance of the arts, which in the
20th century cannot thrive without public patronage.
Whatever improvement occurred in this situation towards the end of the inter-war period can be credited
largely to Karol Szymanowski, to his endeavours in
the field of organization and journalism, and his personal impact on the whole of his generation.

In the first years of independence, the eyes of Pol-
ish musicians and composers remained fixed on the
West, especially Paris whence shone the beacons of
Stravinsky and Ravel, Diaghilev and the open-handed
Duchess de Polignac. Although there were those, like
Feliks Nowowiejski, Witold Maliszewski, the talented
Eugeniusz Morawski who returned to Poland, this was
only a trickle in comparison with the stream west-
wards. Some of these artists remained there for good:
Alexander Tansman melted into the Paris scene and
enriched modern French music with his original talent;
Ludomir Michał Rogowski settled in Yugoslavia; fa-
mous virtuosi, like Ignacy Paderewski, Artur Rubinstein, Józef Hofmann, Bronisław Huberman, Ada Sari,
Paweł Klecki and others appeared at concerts all over
the world and paid only rare visits to their country.
The young flocked to Paris to brush up the skills and
knowledge of contemporary music, Szymanowski's ge-

nius having opened their eyes to the provincialism and backwardness of musical life and craftsmanship in Poland. In Paris they made up these arrears under Paul Dukas, Vincent d'Indy and, above all, Nadia Boulanger.

In 1926 an enterprising young composer, Piotr Perkowski, formed the *Association des Jeunes Musiciens Polonais à Paris* which became a vigorous little organization and established contacts with the French music world. Among its members were Grażyna Bacewicz, Jerzy Fitelberg (son of Grzegorz), Alfred Gradstein, Tadeusz Zygfryd Kassern, Stefan Kisielewski, Anna Maria Klechniowska, Michał Kondracki, Szymon Laks, Felix Łabuński, Roman Maciejewski, Jan Maklakiewicz, Zygmunt Mycielski, Witold Rudziński, Kazimierz Sikorski, Michał Spisak, Antoni Szałowski, Tadeusz Szeligowski, Stanisław Wiechowicz and Bolesław Woytowicz, and a large number of pianists, violinists, singers etc. who made up a large and tight-knit artistic community.

The Europeanization of Polish music, craved by the "Young Poland" composers, and given such splendid shape by Szymanowski, was an ideal espoused by the whole of the younger generation. But as a result of their Paris studies it was the prevailing neo-classical current which they brought back with them, one totally alien to the nature of Szymanowski who was basically an artist in the romantic mould. This may make it less astonishing that Chopin's greatest successor, a composer of immense authority and personal influence, failed to create a school. He flashed on to the empty firmament of our music like a meteor and disappeared, leaving behind no disciples or imitators. Nevertheless the trail he blazed proved magnificently rewarding: what his juniors learned abroad brought an unprecedented improvement in the practice of composition and, apart from a considerable broadening of horizons, laid the foundation for the further creative development of Polish music.

Everyone of any progressive bent in the music world rallied to Szymanowski and the ideas he professed and propagated in various writings, such as The Music of the Highlands (1924), The Roads and Wildernesses of Contemporary Music (1925), or The Educational Role of Musical Culture in Society (1930). His supporters also included the musicologists, historians and ethnographers of a dynamic new field of scholarship launched at the end of the 19th century by the researches in old Polish music of Józef Surzyński (1851—1919) and Aleksander Poliński (1845—1916). In the early 20th century, such studies were pushed into a more scientific direction by a group of musicologists educated abroad, mainly in Germany.

These were Henryk Opieński (1870—1942), Wacław Gieburowski (1878—1943), Józef Reiss (1879—1956), Alicja Simon (1879—1957), Adolf Chybiński (1880—1952), Zdzisław Jachimecki (1882—1953), Łucjan Kamieński (1885—1964) and Ludwik Bronarski (b. 1890), and they succeeded in getting Poland's first chairs of musicology established in Cracow (1911, Jachimecki), Lvov (1912, Chybiński) and Poznań (1922, Kamieński). They trained a large number of young researchers who undertook wide-ranging projects in the history of Polish music, both written and vernacular. Periodicals also began to flourish, and the Polish Music Publishing Society was formed to bring out old as well as contemporary scores. A further impetus came from the work of critics and writers interested in the new music, such as Mateusz Gliński (b. 1892), conductor, composer and musicologist, founder of the monthly Muzy-ka (1924—38), or Konstanty Régamey (b. 1907), a distinguished composer, critic and linguist, who started the review Muzyka Polska (1937).

Nevertheless modern music still remained something of a fringe activity with only a small audience. It had a relative ally in the Warsaw Opera, thanks partly to the policy pursued by Emil Młynarski, its manager in the years 1919—29, who did not flinch from putting on Strauss, Stravinsky, Janáček, Ravel, Szymanowski, Różycki, Statkowski, and the like.

The Warsaw Opera was also lucky in its company. Until 1925, the assistant conductor was Artur Rodziński, and the singers included Helena Zboińska-Ruszkowska, Matylda Polińska-Lewicka, Janina Korolewicz-Waydowa, Ewa Bandrowska-Turska, Maria Mokrzycka, Ignacy Dygas, Wanda Wermińska, Stanisław Gruszczyński, Aleksander Michałowski, and many others equally talented. The Poznań Opera under the direction of Piotr Stermich-Valcrociata and Zygmunt Latoszewski was only a short step behind. The Warsaw and Poznań Philharmonics, on the other hand, laboured under great financial difficulties which made it impossible to maintain a consistently high standard despite some memorable concerts. In the years 1925—34, the First Conductor of the Warsaw Philharmonic was Grzegorz Fitelberg who left to organize the symphony orchestra of the Polish Radio, the best there was in Poland in the inter-war period.

An idea which aroused the eager response of the general public was Jerzy Żurawlew's notion of holding a regular competition for performances of Chopin. The object was to propagate his music and show its world importance. The 1st Frédéric Chopin International Piano Competition was duly staged in Warsaw in 1927, one of the first such events anywhere. Since then the Chopin Competitions, organized every five years, have been recognized throughout the music world as one of the most exacting and supreme tests for pianists and long ago acquired a significance far beyond the original intentions, having become not only a focus for the Chopin cult, but also a considerable influence on the development of piano playing in Poland. The prize-winners at the 1927 Competition were Lev Oborin (Soviet Union), Stanisław Szpinalski (Poland), Róża Etkin (Poland), Grigori Ginsburg (Soviet Union) and Henryk Sztompka (Poland), and one of the runners-up was Dmitri Shostakovich. At the 2nd Competition, in 1932, the prizes went to Alexander Uninsky (France), Imré Ungár (Hungary), Bolesław Kon (Poland), Abram Lufer (Soviet Union) and Louis Kentner (Hungary). In 1937, the first two places were taken by Jakub Żak and Rosa Tamarkina of the Soviet Union, the third by Witold Małcużyński (Poland), and the other two by Monique de la Bruchollerie (France) and Jan Ekier (Poland). On the jury were such distinguished pianists as Emil Sauer, Magda Tagliaferro, Isidore Philipp, Wilhelm Backhaus and Harry Neuhaus. World War II cut off the Competition in full stride.

It did the same to the Henryk Wieniawski International Violin Competition, inaugurated in 1935 on the 100th anniversary of the birth of the great Polish violinist. The first aroused great interest with an entry of 160 musicians from all over the world. The jury included Jenö Hubay, Jacques Thibaud, Georg Kulenkampff and Bronisław Huberman. The general standard was very high, the awards going to Ginette Neveu (France), David Oistrakh (Soviet Union), Henry

Temianka (Great Britain), two Polish violinists, Ida Haendel and Bronisław Gimpel; among those commended was Grażyna Bacewicz, who was to make much more of a mark as a composer.

The war's brutal impact on all spheres of life also arrested the momentum which music had so promisingly developed. In the 1930s a large number of talented and foreign-trained composers had appeared and, for the first time in centuries, given Polish music the chance of getting on terms with the rest of the world. This was made manifest by the confrontation that took place at the 17th International Festival of Contemporary Music held in Warsaw in April 1939, just four and a half months before Nazi Germany invaded Poland, when works by Stanisław Wiechowicz, Bolesław Woytowicz, Michał Kondracki, Antoni Szałowski and Jerzy Fitelberg were performed. Of the young composers who made their bow in the thirties or just before the war, Witold Lutosławski, Roman Palester, Piotr Perkowski and Michał Spisak stood out as names to watch. For all of them, the war meant, at best, a five-year hiatus at the very time when they should have been reaching their peak, the evaporation of whatever reputation they might already have gained, and in many cases the destruction of all they had written.

The war sacked homes, concert halls and opera houses, scattered orchestras and musicians, reduced manuscripts, documents and antiquities to cinders. It might have seemed that there would be precious little time for the arts when the main concern was merely survival. Yet it was the years of Nazi occupation that revealed once again the transcendentally social and national role of music. They wrote a separate and significant chapter in its history in Poland.

RECORDINGS BY "POLSKIE NAGRANIA — MUZA" OF
POLISH MUSIC FROM THE YEARS 1900—39 (selection)

Ignacy Jan Paderewski: Piano Works
    Ryszard Bakst, piano. XL 0097

Ignacy Jan Paderewski: *Polish Fantasia* for piano and orchestra (op. 19)
    Regina Smendzianka (piano), Symphony Orchestra of the National Philharmonic, conducted by Stanisław Wisłocki. XL 0114

Ignacy Jan Paderewski: *Piano Concerto in A Minor* (op. 17)
    Barbara Hesse-Bukowska (piano), Polish Radio Grand Symphony Orchestra, conducted by Jan Krenz. XL 0196

Ignacy Jan Paderewski: *Sonata in E flat minor* (op. 21); *Variations and Fugue in E flat Minor* (op. 23)
    Andrzej Stefański, piano. XL 0570

Mieczysław Karłowicz: *Violin Concerto in A Major;* symphonic poem *Smutna opowieść* (A Sad Tale)
    Wanda Wiłkomirska (violin), Symphony Orchestra of the National Philharmonic, conducted by Witold Rowicki and Stanisław Wisłocki. XL 0179

Mieczysław Karłowicz: Symphonic poems *Stanisław i Anna Oświęcimowie* (Stanisław and Anna Oświęcim) and *Epizod na maskaradzie* (Episode at a Masked Ball)
    Symphony Orchestra of the National Philharmonic, conducted by Stanisław Wisłocki. XL 0269

Mieczysław Karłowicz: Symphonic poems *Odwieczne pieśni* (Immemorial Songs) and *Rapsodia litewska* (Lithuanian Rhapsody)
    Symphony Orchestra of the National Philharmonic, conducted by Stanisław Wisłocki. XL 0290

Mieczysław Karłowicz: Collected Songs
    Andrzej Hiolski (baritone), Jerzy Marchwiński (piano). XL 0862

71

Ludomir Różycki: *Ballad* for piano and orchestra (op. 2)
Barbara Hesse-Bukowska (piano), Polish Radio Grand Symphony Orchestra, conducted by Jan Krenz. XL 0196

Ludomir Różycki: Symphonic poems *Stańczyk, Bolesław Śmiały* (Boleslaus the Bold) and *Anhelli*
Symphony Orchestra of the Poznań Philharmonic, conducted by Robert Satanowski. XL 0225

Karol Szymanowski: *Variations in B minor* (op. 10); *Preludes* (op. 1); *Variations in B flat minor* (op. 3)
Tadeusz Żmudziński, piano. XL 0335

Karol Szymanowski: *Maski* (Masks) (op. 34); *2nd Sonata* (op. 21)
Andrzej Stefański, piano. XL 0463

Karol Szymanowski: *1st Violin Concerto, 4th Concertante Symphony*
Wanda Wiłkomirska (violin), Jan Ekier (piano), Symphony Orchestra of the National Philharmonic, conducted by Witold Rowicki. XL 0116

Karol Szymanowski: *1st Violin Concerto; 2nd Violin Concerto*
Wanda Wiłkomirska (violin), Charles Treger (violin), Symphony Orchestra of the National Philharmonic, conducted by Witold Rowicki and Robert Satanowski. XL 0383

Karol Szymanowski: *Stabat Mater*, oratorio; *3rd Symphony*
Stefania Woytowicz (soprano), Krystyna Szczepańska (alto), Andrzej Hiolski (baritone), Choir and Orchestra of the National Philharmonic, conducted by Witold Rowicki. XL 0149

Karol Szymanowski: *Król Roger* (King Roger), opera in 3 acts
Soloists, Choir and Orchestra of the Grand Theatre in Warsaw, conducted by Mieczysław Mierzejewski. XL 0250—0251

Karol Szymanowski: Three Mazurkas op. 50 (No 2, 3, 7)
Sviatoslav Richter, piano. XL 0037

Karol Szymanowski: Twenty Mazurkas (op. 50)
Barbara Hesse-Bukowska, piano. XL 0102

Karol Szymanowski: *Harnasie* (Highland Robbers), ballet
Choir and Orchestra of the Grand Theatre in Warsaw, conducted by Bohdan Wodiczko. XL 0249

Karol Szymanowski: Selected Works, casette (5 records and album)

Stanisław Wiechowicz: *Chmiel* (Hops), wedding dance for orchestra
  Polish Radio Grand Symphony Orchestra, conducted by Jan Krenz. XL 0238

Tadeusz Szeligowski: *Epitaph on the Death of Karol Szymanowski* for string orchestra
  Polish Radio Grand Symphony Orchestra, conducted by Jan Krenz. XL 0238

Bolesław Szabelski: *Toccata* for orchestra
  Polish Radio Grand Symphony Orchestra, conducted by Jan Krenz. XL 0238

Antoni Szałowski: *Overture* for orchestra
  Polish Radio Grand Symphony Orchestra, conducted by Jan Krenz. XL 0238

Piotr Perkowski: *Nocturne* for orchestra
  Polish Radio Grand Symphony Orchestra, conducted by Jan Krenz. XL 0238

IV. CATCHING UP WITH EUROPE – SECOND ATTEMPT

Reconstruction of Music after World War II; State Patronage and Development of Music Life; Music up to 1955, Outstanding Figures, First Successes; Distinguished Performers; Folk Music; Development and Role of Musicology

During World War II Polish culture suffered losses on a scale quite beyond anything in its entire history. They were due not only to the fierce hostilities that twice swept across the whole country but above all to the systematic pursuance of the Nazis' goal of wiping out Poland as a nation. Destruction of the intelligentsia, liquidation of the whole of secondary and higher education, dissolution of organizations of any kind, banning of the arts, closing of theatres, operas and concert-halls, were all steps aimed at reducing the Polish people to the level of helots. Their answer was a widespread resistance movement which also extended to the whole sphere of the mind as well as armed struggle. A clandestine school system was organized, learning and art were pursued in secret, concerts and drama were performed underground, all in defiance of persecutions and reprisals. Thus was preserved a sense of the continuity of life, social ties and national culture. If major achievement was, for obvious reasons, unlikely to come of such conditions, the occupation years were a forceful lesson in the unifying role and significance of art. It became one of the main foundations on which the reconstruction and development of Polish music were based in 1945 under a new socio-political system.

In fact work had started long before the termination of hostilities in the areas liberated from Nazi rule, often right behind the front lines. What was involved was not just physical reconstruction; there was also the whole problem of the place of music in the new context. It had to be given every opportunity and encouragement, its entire fabric, its organizations and institutions, revived or built anew. The principle of wide-ranging state patronage, adopted from the outset and most obviously reflected in the establishment of a Ministry of Culture and Art, made it possible to bring orchestras, philharmonics, operas and conservatoires into being. It is true that they were handicapped at first by the most primitive facilities, but there were more of them than before the war. As early as 1945, there were already 12 symphony orchestras (including two radio orchestras and four philharmonics) and the number grew in subsequent years. At the same time, three opera houses were opened — in Poznań, Bytom and Wrocław. Music schools, organizations and associations were revived and found support in the planned policy of the government.

The role of main cultural centre now passed to Cracow, which had had the good fortune to emerge from the war relatively unscathed. It was there accordingly that the Polish Music Press was founded three weeks before victory in Europe and went on to play a very signal role in the development of contemporary Polish music. At its head was placed Tadeusz Ochlewski, co-founder of the prewar Polish Music Publishing Society. It was in Cracow, too, that a national Composers' Congress was held in the autumn of 1945. It formed the Polish Composers' Union and Piotr Perkowski, whose organizing abilities had been demonstrated in the days of the Paris Association, was elected President. Though membership was on the small side the Union soon became one of the main driving forces in Polish music, a fact worth stressing, since the Polish music world had been severely sapped by the war. Many of its members were dead (for example the composers, Józef Koffler, murdered by the Nazis, and Roman Padlewski, killed during the Warsaw Rising, and the musicologists, Seweryn Barbag, Helena Dorabialska, Jerzy Freiheiter, Wacław Gieburowski, to name only a few); many others were scattered around the world (Jerzy Fitelberg, Mateusz Gliński, Tadeusz Z. Kassern, Michał Kondracki, Szymon Laks, Felix R. Łabuński, Roman Maciejewski, Michał Spisak, Antoni Szałowski, Alexander Tansman and Konstanty Régamey who had had time to settle down in Poland). Some had left before the war; others were stranded by its course.

A companion event to the Composers' Congress was the 1st Festival of Polish Contemporary Music at which a number of works, for the most part written during the war, were performed for the first time. Another immediate result of the Congress was the foundation of the fortnightly Ruch Muzyczny. At the same time, efforts were made to re-open the international contacts, official and private, severed as a result of the war. From this point of view it was a great boon that the Polish cultural attachés in Moscow and New York happened to be connected with music: the musicologist Zofia Lissa and the composer Tadeusz Zygfryd Kassern.

In 1946, the Polish section of the International Society for Contemporary Music (SIMC) was revived. At the same time, representatives of the music world visited Britain, France and Switzerland to establish contacts. One direct result was a series of concerts of contemporary Polish music in London at which Szymanowski's *Harnasie* and chamber music, Kassern's *Concerto for Strings,* and Wawrzyniec Żuławski's *Quintet* were performed and well received. A similar success was scored by Polish composers at the 1946 Festival of Contemporary Music in London. Compositions by Grażyna Bacewicz, Konstanty Régamey, Witold Lutosławski and others were also heard in Paris, when a series of concerts were organized to mark the 20th anniversary of the establishment of the *Association des Jeunes Musiciens Polonais à Paris.* Good work was also done by Grzegorz Fitelberg who spent the war years in South America and, en route back to Poland, conducted a number of concerts in Scandinavia featuring works by young Polish composers.

This far from complete list of performances abroad of contemporary Polish music in the first postwar year is evidence both of a vigorous drive to capture Europe's main music centres — as though to demonstrate how Polish culture had triumphed over the Nazis' attempts to eradicate it — and of an international audience for Polish music. Though subsequently this interest and traffic tailed off, they have taken on a new and redoubled lease of life in recent years. The country's burgeoning music life began to absorb composers to an ever greater degree, though in 1945 and 1946 both their scope and the performance potential were still limited. In the summer of 1947, Grzegorz Fitelberg returned to Poland for good to take charge of the Polish Radio Symphony Orchestra in Katowice, formed two years earlier by Witold Rowicki.

His appointment was a fateful one, for Fitelberg was not only an excellent conductor. As Witold Lutosławski said of him many years later:

He was a figure of particular importance to all Polish composers of my generation. ...It was thanks to him that we were introduced to contemporary music in our youth. He rendered immense services to its performance and propagation — was a true pioneer. As a result it was the dream of every upcoming composer to have his new orchestral works conducted by Fitelberg. It was the same with me. My real début — I say real because earlier performances of my orchestral works were of no consequence — was conducted by Grzegorz Fitelberg. It was my *Symphonic Variations,* first played on the Polish Radio and then at the Wawel Festival in 1939. Fitelberg took great pains with this kind of music. He had a passionate dedication to the cause which gave him a tremendous influence on the young generation of composers. It is hard to conceive today how very deterring was the environment in which we then worked and how meagre were the opportunities of modern music in Poland... Among the postwar performances of my works which I shall remember to the end of my life I include the first performance of my *1st Symphony* by the Radio Orchestra under Fitelberg. It was an enormous encouragement for me, still a young composer then, with only one full-scale work to his name. Fitelberg's enthusiasm and commitment, his battle to get this piece played — it remained more or less incomprehensible to most of the musicians in the orchestra — were tremendously important to my further evolution as a composer. (Tadeusz Kaczyński, *Rozmowy z Witoldem Lutosławskim* (Talking to Witold Lutosławski), PWM 1973, pp. 124—126).

The remarkable talent of this conductor and his enthusiasm for contemporary music was a great blessing to Polish composers for many years, since under him the Polish Radio Symphony Orchestra soon attained a very high standard and devoted much of its repertoire to contemporary Polish music. It was in Katowice that the Karol Szymanowski Competition for Composers was held in 1948, the first major postwar test of the creative resources at Poland's command.

In the same year the Polish Composers' Union organized an Olympic Music Competition and, soon afterwards, the international Olympic jury in London awarded its gold medal to Zbigniew Turski for his *Olympic Symphony*. Works by Grażyna Bacewicz and Stanisław Wiechowicz won honorary citations. For a long time these were to be the last major international successes for Polish composers resident in Poland.

In 1947, the organization of music life began to crystallize. State patronage was taking an increasingly concrete form, one feature being substantial increases in grants to the arts. At the same time, certain aesthetic concepts regarding the role of the composer and the function of music in a society engaged in building socialism began to be mooted.

At the General Assembly of the Polish Composers' Union in the autumn of 1947, Witold Rudziński talked of "an excessive preoccupation with organizational and administrative matters at the expense of musical and ideological concerns" and declared that "the Union should be a hotbed of ideological discussion whereas I see composers retreating into elitarianism". These words signalled a basic change in views of the role and tasks of music. Six months later, at the International Congress of Composers and Critics in Prague, Professor Zofia Lissa spelled out the issue more specifically in her paper "On the Social Functions of Music". For a number of years she was to be the chief exponent of the aesthetic which now took hold of Polish music.

It would be wrong, however, to think that in this first postwar period, composers' energies were wholly consumed by organizational and, later, ideological problems. On the contrary, the rapid development of all spheres of music life was accompanied by a creative impetus that produced a spate of new works.

The years 1945—48 brought 43 first performances. On the other hand the flow of new talent possessing all the drive of youth was still at a low ebb on account of the wartime hiatus. Although there were nevertheless a number of interesting débuts — e.g. those of Stanisław Wisłocki, Stanisław Prószyński, Jan Krenz, Waldemar Maciszewski, Jerzy Sokorski, Stanisław Skrowaczewski — the years found the interests of most of these musicians turning to the piano or conducting.

The oldest generation, represented by Witold Friemann, Jan Maklakiewicz, Ludomir Różycki, Kazimierz Sikorski, Bolesław Szabelski, Tadeusz Szeligowski and Stanisław Wiechowicz, had to go through a period of adjustment to the new postwar conditions before their creative drive could express itself in new works.

Thus the main role fell to the composers who, though still young, had had time to develop an identity of their own before the war and in some cases display a flash of originality. Most of them, as has already been mentioned, remained under the influence of their studies in Paris, but this did not prevent a great diversity of styles and techniques. It is worth emphasizing that the most promising among their number, such as Witold Lutosławski, Artur Malawski and Roman Palester, owed little or nothing to the school of Nadia Boulanger. As regards style, this first postwar period was a continuation of the course on which Polish music had embarked before 1939. Why, however, was no effort made to follow up the legacy of Szymanowski or the explorations of Koffler? The reason may be the strong counter-pull of those Paris influences and a notion that Szymanowski's aesthetic was out-of-date and his métier, when divorced from his personality, was no longer airworthy in 1945. As for Józef Koffler (1896—1943), the first Polish composer to make interesting and creative use of twelve-note technique, his work was too little known to be a fount of inspiration. In any case few in 1945 could have foreseen that the seed sown by Schönberg would yield such abundant fruit, that it would amount to more than a passing episode and that his ideas, however speculative, were so richly pregnant.

Around 1948, there appeared new developments in the work of many Polish composers. There was the increasingly frequent resort to the cantata form, previously extremely rare; more and more often, too, composers sought inspiration in folk music. At the same time, the exploration of new technical and creative ground lost momentum and composing idioms became simplified.

This was due to the growing influence of an aesthetic promoted by the media of state patronage, which sought the widest possible dissemination of music by ironing out its intricacies so that it could be readily understood by the "man in the street". The cantata, conceived as a more elaborate cousin of the mass song, was thought the most adequate for this purpose. At the same time it was maintained that music should reflect the sweeping transformations in progress in the country and that a national style could be best worked up from folk themes. These three requirements resulted in preference being given to works that aroused strong emotional responses tinged with optimism, employed a traditional language and were thematically related to folklore.

In August 1949, there was held a National Congress of Composers and Music Critics in Łagów at which a formula was laid down for current trends in art defined as socialist realism. Its basic principle was that music, like the other contemporary arts, should express socialist content in a national form.

In the years that followed musicologists and critics tried to define exactly what socialist realism meant in the case of music. These efforts did not, however, bring the expected results and produced a situation none too favourable to creative evolution, at a time when developments elsewhere were setting the course of modern music for years to come.

One result of the Łagów Congress was the formation by three young composers, Tadeusz Baird, Jan Krenz and Kazimierz Serocki, and a music critic, Tadeusz Marek, of "Group 49" which set itself the aim of translating socialist realism into practice and composing music which could both satisfy the average listener and be of technical interest.

The state awards first presented in 1950 seemed to be an official indication of the type of music that was thought to come closest to socialist realism. The winners were Tadeusz Szeligowski, Stanisław Wiechowicz, Grażyna Bacewicz, Alfred Gradstein and Tomasz Kiesewetter and in each case the citation emphasized the folk-music inspiration of their works.

Many cantatas were written in these years, both by younger and older composers. A factor which made it easier to guide their work was that in 1952 the allocation of grants was transferred from the Composers' Union to a special Commission set up at the Ministry of Culture and Art.

There came a tide of stylizations and adaptations of

old music. This was taken by Roman Palester (a new arrangement of Michał Kleofas Ogiński's *Polonaises*) and Andrzej Panufnik (*Divertimento*, based on music by Feliks Janiewicz, *Gothic Concerto* and *Old-Polish Suite*). Jan Krenz deftly reconstructed 18th-century symphonies by Milwid and Dankowski and Stanisław Skrowaczewski composed his *Overture in the Classical Style;* a year later, Tadeusz Baird wrote an *Overture in the Old Style* followed by the suite *Colas Breugnon.* Meanwhile Malawski had composed *Siciliana and Rondo,* and *Sonata on Themes by Janiewicz.* A similar course was followed by Kazimierz Sikorski in the *3rd Symphony.* Finally, in 1953, Stanisław Wisłocki transcribed Franciszek Ścigalski's *Symphony.* All these were escapes from the prevalent aesthetic and thematic canons, often arresting and artistically rewarding but in the long run self-defeating.

In 1949, the first postwar generation of Polish composers made its bow and, through the newly-formed Youth Section of the Polish Composers' Union, gradually assumed the role of an avant-garde. Its members included the likes of Tadeusz Baird, Jan Krenz, Kazimierz Serocki, Andrzej Markowski, Andrzej Dobrowolski, Tadeusz Machl, Włodzimierz Kotoński and Andrzej Koszewski. For the most part, their great asset was an absolute sureness of touch though it was limited to traditional techniques and conventional expression. Insufficient acquaintance with the paths being explored in world music led to sights being confined to considerations of vernacular aspects and national style.

Nevertheless among the younger composers the new idioms were already beginning to catch on and some attempts were even made to use them. One of the first was the *Suite of Preludes* for piano by Kazimierz Serocki, whitten as early as 1952, in which a toying with twelve-note technique can be detected. In any case, by 1953 aesthetic canons were being relaxed. In 1955 Kazimierz Sikorski was elected president of the Polish Composers' Union, Zofia Lissa withdrew into academic work and the National Philharmonic was put in the hands of Bohdan Wodiczko who brought the contemporary masterpieces hitherto unperformed and unknown in Poland into the repertoire. Tadeusz Baird and Kazimierz Serocki mooted the idea of holding an International Festival of Contemporary Music in Warsaw and in October 1956 the "Warsaw Autumn" was born.

At that time, there was still no composer who could claim to stand out among his fellows on the score of popular or critical recognition. There was, however, quite a numerous group of talented artists whose works were beginning to attract increasing notice in the musical world and among the public.

One of these was Artur Malawski (1904—57), who had been prevented by the war from revealing his creative potential. Even his earliest works — *1st Symphony* (written during the war), *Toccata* for orchestra (1947), *Symphonic Études* for piano and orchestra (1948), and *Overture* (1948) — reflected a crystallized personal style based on an informed sifting of the modern vocabulary. It had a classicist bias, but one married to an interest in folk music inspired by Szymanowski's last period. However much this may have conformed with official ideas of the roots of a national style, the fact is that, though the final version of Malawski's *Wierchy* (Mountain Peaks) for solo voices, choir and orchestra, the copybook example of artistic stylization of highland music, dates from 1950, it was first drafted as early as 1944. In any case, his was too strong a personality to toe an orthodox line. In 1949, he wrote *Toccata and Fugue in the Form of Variations* for orchestra, a work as radical in sound as his preceding compositions. A year later came the aforementioned *Wierchy* and a cantata, *Stara baśń* (An Old Tale) after which followed a silence of several years, occupied by teaching work and the development in private of a creative synthesis of style and technique. Of the resulting compositions, *Piano Trio* (1953) was eventually hailed as a landmark in Polish chamber music while the *2nd Symphony* (completed in 1956) is distinguished by an individual maturity of style, radicalism of sound, independent but consummate technique, and emotional intensity. Malawski's last work before his untimely death was the dramatic *Hungaria* for string orchestra, written at the end of 1956.

Witold Lutosławski (b. 1913) had already attracted attention before the war, mainly with his *Symphonic Variations* (1937), with their dazzling instrumentation and interesting harmony, and revealed his most characteristic qualities: sophistication of colour, command of structure and pursuit of a new and logical harmonic system. Most of his prewar output was lost in the Warsaw Rising, so that 1945 may be regarded as a second début. *Variations on a Theme of Paganini* for two pianos, written during the war, a harmonically interesting piece of great brio, won immense success. In *Folk Melodies* for piano, written in 1945, there appeared for the first time an interest in folklore which was later to intertwine with explorations of colour and harmony to produce a stream of music which broke significantly new ground. However, neither these compositions nor the *1st Symphony* (1947) or the *Overture for Strings* (1948) were yet an adequate sample of his talent. For a few years he then concentrated on short instrumental or instrumental-and-vocal pieces, such as *Little Suite* (1950), *Straw Chainlet* (1951), *Bucolics* for piano (1952), *Ten Polish Dances,* etc. Many of them were written for children, but have a distinctive charm and are far from primitive.

With the hindsight afforded by Lutosławski's later achievement, one can see that these miniatures, often inspired by folk music, were exercises in the possibilities of sound and instrumentation. Exploration of interesting rhythm problems was wedded to a feeling for form, a subtlety of tone colour and a sense of musical humour to create a recognizable foretaste of the Lutosławski style. Of works of a larger scale experiments with sound can be heard in *Silesian Triptych* for soprano and orchestra (1951), but only in one, *Concerto for Orchestra,* written in the years 1950—54 and hailed at the time as an outstanding achievement of contemporary Polish music, was an attempt made to knit all this into a coherent whole. On balance, however, the years 1949—55 spelled for Lutosławski (as for Malawski) a standstill in his development, but marked an accumulation of technical resources which was to explode in the mature brilliance and innovation of his subsequent oeuvre.

A very active composer in these years was Grażyna Bacewicz (1913—69). In the intervals of pursuing a distinguished career as a violinist, she wrote music that was an extension of the neo-classicist current. Her style was intimated in three violin sonatas, three violin concertos, *Concerto for String Orchestra*, the *3rd*

String Quartet and several other works; somewhat impersonal, objective, anti-programmatic, finding an outlet in sonata forms; and restrained but superbly competent in its language. Extremely and dangerously prolific, her style took shape very gradually, from work to work. Where her earlier compositions were of an impersonal, anti-Romantic character, close to the objectivist French music of the inter-war period, those of the years 1949—55 were marked by an increasing emotional factor and by a certain radicalization of sound. In 1954, Bacewicz retired from the concert platform but creatively remained as active as ever. In these years, she composed four symphonies, two violin concertos, two string quartets (including the *4th Quartet* which was awarded first prize at the Liège competition in 1951), the ballet *Z chlopa król* (Peasant Turned King), two piano sonatas, and several other works.

Roman Palester (b. 1907) lost most of his compositions in the Warsaw Rising and had to start virtually from scratch, though with a reputation as one of the more original and adventurous talents to have appeared in the thirties. In 1945, at the festival in Cracow, Palester presented the *2nd Symphony* composed during the war. Soon afterwards came performances of ·his *3rd String Quartet* and *Violin Concerto*. These works showed a considerable evolution manifested in a simpler texture, refined harmony and a leaning to romantic feeling. The subsequent: *Serenade* for two flutes and strings (1947), *Trio* (1946), *Nocturne* for strings (1947), *Divertimento* for nine instruments (1947), *3rd Symphony* and the profound *Requiem* (1948), mark succeeding stages. His later works were written abroad and unfortunately are not known to us.

Our knowledge of Andrzej Panufnik (b. 1914) is also limited. After the war he seemed one of the more interesting figures in Polish music. The 1945 Cracow festival presented his *Five Folk Songs* for women's choir and a wind ensemble; and later came *Tragic Overture* written during the war, a quarter-tone *Lullaby* for 29 string instruments and two harps (1947) and *Nocturne* for orchestra (1948) with its elaborate colour. These pieces, together with a few heard before the war, were evidence of a sense of colour and harmony and a plumbing of the new possibilities of the orchestra, quarter-tone scales and the sound material of folk music. Subsequently he produced *Sinfonia Rustica* for eight wind instruments and two string orchestras (1949), *Old-Polish Suite* for strings (1950), *Peace Symphony* for choir and symphony orchestra (1951), *Gothic Concerto* for trumpet and orchestra (1952), *Heroic Overture* for orchestra (1952) and *Quintet* for wind instruments (1953). They represent a wide range of interests, but with the exception of the dramatic *Overture*, they reveal an abatement or even abandonment of his earlier sound explorations. If *Sinfonia Rustica* is an attempt at continuing the experiments with folk music, *Old-Polish Suite* and *Gothic Concerto* are an escape into the stylistic regions of old music.

Among other composers mention should be made first of all of Stanisław Wiechowicz (1893—1963), a remarkably talented and original artist, who probably did not turn his gifts to full account because he concentrated on teaching and choral works. In the latter field, he was, for that matter, Poland's greatest master. The folk suite *Kasia* (Kate, 1946), *Na glinianym wazoniku* (On a Clay Vase) for mixed choir and orchestra (1947) and *Kantata żniwna* (Harvest Canta-ta) for *a cappella* choir (1948) are all examples of in-teresting and creative stylization of folk music, com-bined with richness of colour and harmony. Wiecho-wicz had a profound knowledge of modern techniques, but his tapping of it was restrained by the purpose and nature of most of his works. Even in the twen-ties, he had already been one of the most fervent ad-vocates of the popularization of music, organizing and conducting amateur choirs and writing for them. His grasp of modern music, which he imparted to his pu-pils, was more a result of his voracious and lively in-tellect. Since his main province was vocal or vocal-and-instrumental music, the favoured position en-joyed by the cantata form should have made this a good period for him. However, its general atmo-sphere and his own preoccupation with teaching re-sulted in his being less productive than might have been expected. Apart from some songs and arrange-ments, his output included *Silesian Suite* (1950), *Ro-mantic Cantata* (1954) and two orchestral works, *Po-lish Serenade* and *Old Town Concerto* (1954).

Wiechowicz and Malawski turned Cracow into a flo-urishing centre of education which was to produce ma-ny talented young composers. In Warsaw, on the other hand, the central figure was Kazimierz Si-korski, a distinguished teacher to whom almost the whole postwar generation of composers owe their knowledge. Absorbed by teaching and the affairs of the Composers' Union, he seemed to have little time left for composing, writing a few popular pieces and concertos for wind instruments, and it was not until 1953 that he presented a major work, the *3rd Sym-phony* cast along the lines of a concerto grosso. Echo-

89

ing in form and technique Baroque music, making masterly use of the polyphonic potential of the orchestra, and strongly emotional, it blended his knowledge and interests with the contemporary tendency to "baroquize".

The outstanding exponent of this trend was then Bolesław Szabelski (b. 1896), one of the few disciples of Karol Szymanowski. Szabelski settled in Katowice where he attracted pupils. Though relatively little known previously or perhaps simply not given his due, he made an increasing impact with each new work. The *Third Symphony* (1951), *Festive Overture* (1953), *Concerto Grosso* for orchestra (1954) and *Concertino* for piano and orchestra (1955) crystallized a highly individual style whose features were an inclination towards linear texture, expressiveness, the attainment of uncomplicated sound effects by modern means and original colour. The anti-programme character of his music, its independence of both folklore and neo-classical models, and a polyphonization of symphonic forms deriving from his interest in organ music, made Szabelski a leading representative of a current which re-worked pre-classical idioms. The striking subsequent evolution of this artist, long past his youth, was to give him a prominent position among the most radically-minded avant-garde. His coeval, Tadeusz Szeligowski (1896—1963) took longer to come to the forefront. A composer of great gifts, somewhat eclectic and hackneyed in the use he made of them, he already had a considerable oeuvre to his name from before the war, augmented by *Nocturne for Orchestra* (1947) and the ballet *Paw i dziewczyna* (The Peacock and the Girl, 1948). But it was only in the following years that he gathered steam, composing several orchestral works, chamber music and songs, stylistically diversified but on the traditional side, and continuing his interest in music for the stage. In 1951, he completed the first Polish postwar opera *Bunt żaków* (The Students' Revolt). In 1955 came a second opera *Krakatuk* shortly followed by the beginning of work on the ballet *Mazepa*, the twin peaks of Szeligowski's achievement. He remained faithful to the ideal of a national music addressed to the broad public and tailored to its listening preferences and capacities. Though he showed little interest in the technical problems of modern music, his talent, richness of invention and experience endowed these works with a lasting value.

In the case of Zygmunt Mycielski (b. 1907) and Stefan Kisielewski (b. 1911) — otherwise two very different composers as regards temperament and style — their gifts were now chiefly expressed in journalism. Although of varying persuasions, both had already taken up the cudgels for the new music before the war. Nevertheless, despite the press of involvement in music criticism and Union affairs, Mycielski produced a number of interesting works: *Five Symphonic Sketches* (1945), *1st Symphony* (1947) and *Five Songs* to poems by Czesław Miłosz (1947). Though always closely linked with the French music world, he fought shy of its neo-classical influences. Indeed, the strong emotionalism of his music, the quest for a style — personal but at the same time Polish — of his own, a certain reserve towards the latest techniques, but combined with an aesthetic liberalism, all bore the distinct stamp of Szymanowski — and Mycielski had, in fact, been of his circle. Such compositions as *Polish Symphony* (1950), *Five Mazovian Songs* for choir and orchestra (1953), *Piano Concerto* (1954), *Six Preludes for Piano* (1954), *New Mazovian Lyrist* for soprano, baritone, choir and orchestra (1955) were a response to the demand for creation of a national style which to some extent corresponded to his own interests; essays in this direction were repeated in a variety of ways in his subsequent works.

For his part Stefan Kisielewski returned to composing in 1949 when he reconstructed the score of his *Concerto for Chamber Orchestra,* written six years earlier but lost. In it and in *2nd Symphony* (1951), *Little Overture* (1953), *Perpetuum mobile* for orchestra (1955) and numerous miniatures for piano, his style was unfurled in full. As he has repeatedly stated, he treats music as a kind of *divertissement,* which has resulted in his eschewing almost completely expression of the romantic type and remaining within the orbit of neo-classicism. An exception are *Twelve Songs* for voice and piano, to poems by K.I. Gałczyński (1954) in which a simple but radical use of sound produces highly lyrical and dramatic effects.

The output of other composers — Witold Friemann, Irena Garztecka, Alfred Gradstein, Tomasz Kiesewetter, Piotr Perkowski, Stefan B. Poradowski, Witold Rudziński, Zbigniew Turski, Bolesław Woytowicz — faded into the background of music life as a whole, although there were a number of worthwhile works — Woytowicz's cantata *Prorok* (The Prophet), Turski's *Violin Concerto,* Perkowski's *Nocturne,* or Rudziński's *Quintet.*

In 1949, the first postwar crop of composers appeared on the scene, soon winning recognition and advancing to prominent positions, though thanks not only to their undoubted gifts but also to many of the composers of the elder generation having fetched up abroad. Nevertheless the later evolution of Baird and Serocki, for example, indicates this early acclaim was fully justified. It grew when in 1950, together with Jan Krenz, they formed "Group 49" with a certain ideological programme (though none too precisely enunciated) which was a positive attempt to meet the requirements of socialist realism. It was, however, short-lived, which shows that the ideological ties among its members were of a superficial nature.

Tadeusz Baird (b. 1928) made his début with an interesting *Sinfonietta* (1949), and his other early works include *1st Symphony* (1950), the *Colas Breugnon* Suite (1951), *Concerto for Orchestra* (1953) and *Lyric Suite* for soprano and orchestra (1953), all of which distinctly bespoke an individual style and indicated the direction in which he was evolving. The feature of Baird's music is an ecstatic emotionalism which at first verged on the late-Romantic monumental symphony before crystallizing into a lyrical expression abounding in invention and subtle instrumental effects. Its vocabulary drew on the whole range then available, from archaism, through modern symphonic forms and primitive vernacularism, to experiments (still gingerly) with dodecaphonist technique. It seems likely, however, that these were all trial runs aimed at finding the language best suited to the articulation of his lyric genius. For both now and later the technical lures of the avant-garde left Baird rather cold, and he was content merely to develop an individual style which went down very well with the public.

Kazimierz Serocki (b. 1922), who also began with monumental and highly dramatic forms, was more radical in his means. He was later to destroy a considerable part of his youthful output, considering it too crude. Of what he preserved mention is due to *1st Symphony* (1952), *2nd Symphony* for choir and orchestra, two cantatas and a number of piano pieces. There were two separate currents in Serocki's work. One was applied music, including some excellent film and theatre scores, which was fairly conventional. The other answered an inner need, and an important role in it was played by technical inventiveness and a passion for experiment. Examples are a *Suite of Preludes* (1952), *Piano Sonata* (1955) and others in which Serocki made increasingly bold play with the dodecaphonist technique, a rare venture in these years.

Jan Krenz (b. 1926) played a less important role than the other two members of "Group 49", mainly because he eventually devoted himself almost exclusively to conducting. In 1953, after the death of Grzegorz Fitelberg, Krenz succeeded him as head of the Polish Radio Grand Symphony Orchestra and had little time left for composing. Until then he had written a number of works of value, such as *1st Symphony* (1949), *Suite of Nocturnes* for orchestra (1950), *Concertino* for piano and orchestra (1952), *Rhapsody* for strings, xylophone, tom-tom, kettle-drums and celesta (1952), which revealed a rich invention, dramatic talent, mastery of instrumentation and technical ingenuity.

Krenz and Serocki — both pupils of Kazimierz Sikorski — were also talented pianists, but chose a different career. Other young composers-conductors were faced with a similar choice. For the most part, in spite of often considerable composing gifts and following interesting débuts or even some few years of success, they settled for conducting. Such was the case with

Stanisław Skrowaczewski, now a distinguished and well-known conductor working in the United States, Stanisław Wisłocki, Andrzej Markowski, Henryk Czyż, Andrzej Cwojdziński, and others.

Among the other composers who made their bow in the first postwar decade, worth noting are Włodzimierz Kotoński (b. 1925) who veered between neo-classicism and interest in highland folklore, Andrzej Dobrowolski (b. 1921), to whom the Polish Composers' Union owes much, Tadeusz Machl (b. 1922), author of interesting organ concertos and numerous symphonic works, Andrzej Koszewski (b. 1922), Tadeusz Paciorkiewicz (b. 1916) and Witold Szalonek (b. 1927).

In spite of the ideological arguments and conflicts within the composing world, music life developed very vigorously. State patronage made possible the realization of many projects, festivals and competitions. In addition to the already mentioned 1945 festival in Cracow, a Festival of Slavonic Music was held in 1947, a Festival of Polish Folk Music in 1949, and two big festivals of Polish music in Warsaw in 1951 and 1955. Annual state awards for music were established in 1950, various musical institutions were set up or expanded, and composers' and performers' competitions were staged.

The abundance and scale of music life soon surpassed the prewar level, though various features dating from the twenties and thirties were retained and developed. As early as May 1945 the Chopin Institute (established in 1934) was revived. Renamed the Chopin Society (TiFC) in 1950 it organized the first of the Chopin Festivals in Duszniki in 1946 and in 1949 it was put in charge of the resumed Chopin International Piano Competitions.

The 4th Competition, the first after the war, aroused immense public interest. The international jury, which included Magda Tagliaferro, Marguerite Long, Lazare Lévy and Lev Oborin, awarded the first prize to Halina Czerny-Stefańska (Poland) and Bella Davidovich (USSR). Among the runners-up were Barbara Hesse-Bukowska, Waldemar Maciszewski, Władysław Kędra, Ryszard Bakst, Zbigniew Szymonowicz, Regina Smendzianka and Tadeusz Żmudziński, who were soon to climb and remain in the first flight of Polish pianists and become well known on concert stages all over the world. The 5th Chopin Competition, in 1955, was a triumph for Adam Harasiewicz, and other Poles among the prize-winners were Lidia Grychtołówna and Andrzej Czajkowski.

The Henryk Wieniawski International Competitions were also resumed, but in Poznań. In 1952, the first two prizes were awarded to Igor Oistrakh (USRR) and Wanda Wiłkomirska (Poland). Three young Polish violinists, Edward Statkiewicz, Igor Iwanow and Henryk Palulis, were commended.

Young Polish performers also scored at competitions abroad, e.g. Wanda Wiłkomirska (violin) and Irena Lewińska (singer) at Geneva, 1946, Jerzy S. Adamczewski (singer) at Geneva, 1947, Alina Bolechowska (singer) at Leipzig, 1950, Barbara Hesse-Bukowska (piano) in Paris, 1954, Stefania Woytowicz (singer) at Prague, 1954, Andrzej Hiolski (singer) at Toulouse, 1954, Edmund Kossowski (singer) at Toulouse, 1954, and Jerzy Katlewicz (conductor) at Besançon, 1955. An active part in music life was also played by artists who had already made a reputation before the war: the pianists, Raul Koczalski (1885—1948), Stanisław Szpinalski (1901—57), Henryk Sztompka (1901—64) and Zbigniew Drzewiecki

Mieczysław Tomaszewski, director of the Polish Music Press (left), and Hieronim Feicht (1894—1967), the distinguished musicologist and historian of Polish music

Tadeusz Ochlewski, founder of the Polish Music Press and its director from 1945 to 1965

Maciej Kamieński (1734—1821); author of *Misery Made Happy*, the first comic opera in Polish

Wojciech Bogusławski (1757—1829), foun of Poland's first professional theatre

Józef Elsner (1769—1854), composer and conductor, founder of Warsaw's first music conservatoire, teacher of Frédéric Chopin

Karol Kurpiński (1785—1857), composer opera conductor, director of the War Opera in the years 1824—40

Frédéric Chopin (1810—49), Poland's greatest composer, author of peerless piano masterpieces (after a lithograph by Nicolas-Eustache Maurin, in the collections of the Frédéric Chopin Society)

Żelazowa Wola, Chopin's birthplace, now a museum. In the summer season, Chopin recitals are given there by outstanding Polish and foreign pianists

Stanisław Moniuszko (1819—72), distinguished composer, the creator of Polish national opera

On 20 November 1965, the curtain was raised for the first time in Warsaw's rebuilt Grand Theatre, first opened in 1833 and destroyed by the Nazis in 1939. The production was the *Haunted Manor* by Stanisław Moniuszko, a composer whose whole life was linked with the Grand Theatre

Henryk Wieniawski (1835—80), composer and famous violin virtuoso

Mieczysław Karłowicz, (1876—1909), Poland's great composer of symphonic music

Karol Szymanowski (1882—1937), Poland's greatest composer of the first half of the 20th century, the creator of a modern national style, who exerted a fundamental influence on the further development of Polish music

The Warsaw Philharmonic, opened in 1901, was the most important centre of music life in Poland. Its building, destroyed during the hostilities in 1939 (above), was reopened in 1945 and became the seat of the National Philharmonic (below). It is here that the annual "Warsaw Autumn" International Festivals of Contemporary Music and the International Chopin Piano Competitions are held, and the most distinguished Polish and foreign musicians appear

Bohdan Wodiczko, outstanding Polish conductor, rendered great services to the development of the National Philharmonic and the Grand Theatre. As a teacher, he educated many talented young musicians

Jan Krenz, conductor and artistic manager of Polish Radio Grand Symphony Orchestra in Katowice in the years 1953—68, subsequently director of the Grand Theatre in Warsaw

Witold Rowicki, founder and conductor of the Polish Radio Grand Symphony Orchestra, subsequently (from 1950) director of the National Philharmonic Symphony Orchestra

Tadeusz Szeligowski (1896—1963), composer and teacher, author of *The Students' Revolt*, the first Polish opera written after the war

Kazimierz Sikorski, composer and educator, teacher of a whole generation of contemporary Polish composers, seen during a class in harmony at the Warsaw College of Music

Grażyna Bacewicz (1913—69), author of numerous symphonic and chamber works, violin concertos and stage music

Nadia Boulanger, the famous French professor of music, teacher of several generations of Polish composers, shown lecturing at Warsaw's College of Music during a visit in 1967. Standing in the background is Zygmunt Mycielski

Witold Lutosławski, Poland's most eminent contemporary composer, author of numerous works performed and acclaimed all over the world ▶

Andrzej Markowski, distinguished conductor whose art and rich experience have been a great help to young Polish avant-garde composers

Bolesław Szabelski, composer and teacher working in Katowice. In 1958, he surprised the public by radically changing his style and joining the young avant-garde

Henryk Czyż, outstanding symphony and opera conductor, for several years a close collaborator of Krzysztof Penderecki; conducted the first performances of *St. Luke Passion* and the opera *The Devils of Loudun*

Kazimierz Serocki, distinguished composer, one of the initiators and co-organizers of the "Warsaw Autumn" Festivals

(K. H. Wörner) — "a modern composer [who writes] modern beautiful music" Tadeusz Baird — one of the initiators of the "Warsaw Autumn" Festivals

Włodzimierz Kotoński, who in some fifteen years has travelled all the way from folk inspiration to the extreme musical avant-garde; now the head of the Electronic Music Studio in the Warsaw College of Music

Zbigniew Drzewiecki (1890—1971), distinguished pianist and teacher, educator of several generations of pianists and prize-winners at the Chopin Competitions

Ostrogski Palace in Warsaw, seat of the Frédéric Chopin Society

Witold Małcużyński, world-famous Polish pianist (right), talking to Jan Ekier, pianist, educator and leading authority on Chopin

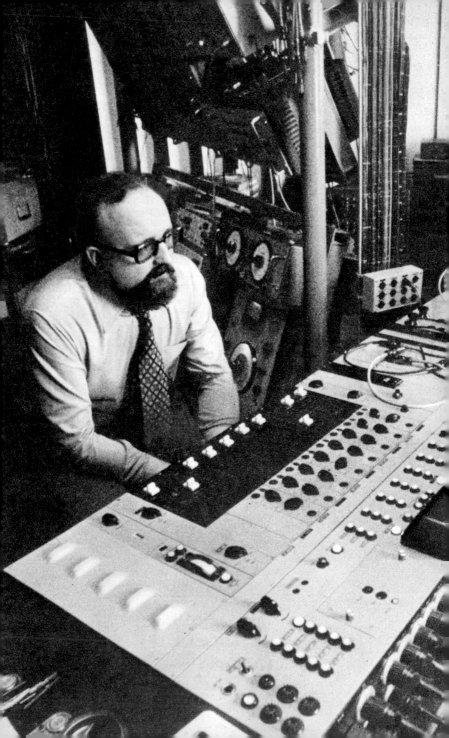

Krzysztof Penderecki, the best known of Poland's younger avant-garde composers, author of *Threnody for the Victims of Hiroshima, St. Luke Passion, The Devils of Loudun,* at work in the Experimental Studio of the Polish Radio in Warsaw

Henryk Mikołaj Górecki, distinguished avant-garde composer noted for the crispness and expressiveness of his music

Witold Szalonek, one of the boldest experimenters in the field of new instrumental sounds, particularly in wind instruments

Wojciech Kilar, author of symphonic works hailed at "Warsaw Autumn" Festivals, and of excellent film scores

Zbigniew Rudziński, one of the leading representatives of the youngest generation of Polish composers

Tomasz Sikorski, distinguished avan garde composer, is continuing family tradition started by his fath Kazimierz Sikorski

Zygmunt Krauze, composer a pianist, founder of the well-kno avant-garde "Music Workshop"

(1890—1971), the violinists, Eugenia Umińska and Irena Dubiska and the singers, Ewa Bandrowska-Turska and Wanda Wermińska, to mention just the most distinguished.

These musicians and an increasing spate of guest appearances by foreign ones were the main attractions of concert life in the postwar years. Its development was made possible by the formation of several new orchestras. The best of them was the Polish Radio Grand Symphony Orchestra under Grzegorz Fitelberg and Jan Krenz. Two others which stood out were the Symphony Orchestra of the Bydgoszcz Broadcasting Station, directed in 1945—55 by Arnold Rezler, and the Polish Radio Orchestra and Choir in Cracow, organized in 1947.

The Warsaw Philharmonic was revived in 1947 and three years later was placed in the hands of the distinguished conductor, Witold Rowicki. Under his energetic management its young ensemble soon attained a high standard. In 1955, it was renamed the National Philharmonic and moved into the reconstructed hall of the prewar Philharmonic. By then, the rebuilding of the Grand Theatre in Warsaw had been under way for five years. Only its handsome monumental façade, so much a part of the Warsaw tradition, had survived the war.

Another branch of the development of artistic life was exemplified by the establishment in 1949 of the now famous "Mazowsze" song and dance company under the management of Tadeusz Sygietyński and Mira Ziminńska and, in 1953, of a similar ensemble, "Śląsk", directed by Stanisław Hadyna. Both performed the valuable function of giving a lead to the vast number of nascent amateur groups and vindicating the claims made for folk music.

Interest in folklore found strong support in government policy. Before the war there had been centres in Poznań and Warsaw engaged in collecting and recording folk music, but the results of their work were completely destroyed during the war so that in 1945 it was necessary to start from scratch. Great services were rendered by the distinguished musicologists-cum-ethnographers, Marian and Jadwiga Sobieski. Through the efforts of Marian Sobieski (1908—67), a vast national programme of inventarization was launched. Later sponsored by the State Institute of Art (established in 1948), it covered the whole of Poland and yielded nearly 70,000 recordings. This is a unique collection which has saved our musical folk culture, already being swamped by the march of urban civilization, from sinking into oblivion.

This, however, was only a small portion of the problems that Polish musicologists tackled after the war. Of the four centres established at universities (under Adolf Chybiński in Poznań, 1945, Zdzisław Jachimecki in Cracow, 1945, Hieronim Feicht in Wrocław, 1946 and Zofia Lissa in Warsaw, 1948), the Institute of Musicology at Warsaw University soon came to the fore. Because of the acute shortage of staff, the main concern at this time was didactic. In research, the most prominent representatives of this discipline concentrated, above all, on Polish music in the Renaissance and the 19th century and on contemporary problems. Of major importance were the writings of Zofia Lissa in 1948—55 which brought Marxist methodology into musicology. Her passionate commitment to the affairs of contemporary Polish music made her a figure of considerable authority; subsequently she confined herself to teaching and scholarship. In retrospect it is clear that for all the excessive radicalism of her views, she rendered indisputable services to Polish music culture in the first postwar period as an initiator of a number of valuable research projects, educator of several generations of young musicologists, and prolific author of interesting studies, not all of which have dated. Among the other musicologists the most noteworthy were the theorist Józef M. Chomiński and Hieronim Feicht who, following the deaths of Chybiński (in 1952) and Jachimecki (in 1953), became the most distinguished historian of Polish music.

RECORDINGS BY "POLSKIE NAGRANIA — MUZA" OF PO-
LISH MUSIC FROM THE YEARS 1940—55 (selection)

Grażyna Bacewicz: 4th Sonata for violin and piano
Grażyna Bacewicz (violin) and Kiejstut Bacewicz (piano).
XL 0033

Grażyna Bacewicz: Divertimento for strings
Chamber Orchestra of the National Philharmonic, conducted
by Karol Teutsch. XL 0586

Grażyna Bacewicz: Concerto for Orchestra
Symphony Orchestra of the National Philharmonic, conducted by Witold Rowicki. XL 0274

Tadeusz Baird: Colas Breugnon
Polish Radio Grand Symphony Orchestra, conducted by Jan
Krenz. L 0071

Augustyn Bloch: Organ Sonata
Joachim Grubich, organ. XL 0495

Wojciech Kilar: Little Overture
Symphony Orchestra of the Poznań Philharmonic, conducted
by Józef Wiłkomirski. L 0078

Stefan Kisielewski: Danse vive for piano
Andrzej Dutkiewicz, piano. XL 0827

Włodzimierz Kotoński: Quartettino for wind instruments
Quartet of horns. L 0077

Jan Krenz — Antoni Milwid: Concertante Symphony for oboe
and orchestra
Janusz Banaszek (oboe), Symphony Orchestra of the Bydgoszcz Philharmonic, conducted by Zbigniew Chwedczuk,
XL 0231

Jan Krenz: Rhapsody for xylophone, tom-tom, kettle-drums,
celesta and orchestra

Polish Radio Grand Symphony Orchestra, conducted by Jan Krenz. L 0010

Witold Lutosławski: *Symphonic Variations*
Polish Radio Grand Symphony Orchestra, conducted by Grzegorz Fitelberg. L 0009

Witold Lutosławski: *1st Symphony*
Polish Radio Grand Symphony Orchestra, conducted by Jan Krenz. XL 0237

Witold Lutosławski: *Little Suite*
Symphony Orchestra of the Warsaw Philharmonic, conducted by Witold Lutosławski. L 0002

Witold Lutosławski: *Bucolics* for piano
Andrzej Dutkiewicz, piano. XL 0827

Witold Lutosławski: *Tryptyk Śląski* (Silesian Triptych)
Maria Drewniak (soprano), Polish Radio Grand Symphony Orchestra, conducted by Grzegorz Fitelberg. L 0009

Witold Lutosławski: *Concerto for Orchestra*
Symphony Orchestra of the National Philharmonic, conducted by Witold Rowicki. XL 0132

Artur Malawski: *Symphonic Études*
Regina Smendzianka (piano), Symphony Orchestra of the National Philharmonic, conducted by Stanisław Wisłocki. XL 0171

Artur Malawski: *Overture*
Polish Radio Grand Symphony Orchestra, conducted by Jan Krenz. XL 0238

Artur Malawski: *Trio*
Cracow Trio. XL 0574

Zygmunt Mycielski: *Polish Symphony*
Orchestra of Polish Radio in Cracow, conducted by Jerzy Gert. L 0099

Tadeusz Paciorkiewicz: *Sonata for Organ*
Joachim Grubich, organ. XL 0495

Andrzej Panufnik: *Tragic Overture; Gothic Concerto*
Orchestra of the Warsaw Philharmonic, conducted by Witold Rowicki. L 0208

Andrzej Panufnik: *Old-Polish Suite*
Polish Radio Grand Symphony Orchestra, conducted by Jan Krenz. L 0207

Kazimierz Serocki: *Suite for Four Trombones*
Quartet of the Warsaw Philharmonic. L 0077

Kazimierz Sikorski: *Concerto for Horn and Small Orchestra*
Edwin Golnik (horn), Orchestra of the Warsaw Philharmonic, conducted by Witold Rowicki. L 0208

Michał Spisak: *Toccata*
Polish Radio Grand Symphony Orchestra, conducted by Jan Krenz. L 0060

Michał Spisak: *Suite for String Orchestra*
Symphony Orchestra of the State Philharmonic in Bucharest, conducted by Mircea Basarab. L 0096

Bolesław Szabelski: *Concerto Grosso; Étude*
Polish Radio Grand Symphony Orchestra, conducted by Jan Krenz. XL 0329

Antoni Szałowski: *Trio*
The Warsaw Reed Trio. XL 0813

Tadeusz Szeligowski: *Concerto for Piano and Orchestra*
Halina Siedzieniewska (piano), Symphony Orchestra of the National Philharmonic, conducted by Stanisław Wisłocki. XL 0205

Tadeusz Szeligowski: *Sonatina*
Stanisław Szpinalski, piano. L 0152

Zbigniew Turski: *Violin Concerto*
Tadeusz Wroński (violin), Symphony Orchestra of the National Philharmonic, conducted by Stanisław Wisłocki. XL 0140

Zbigniew Turski: *2nd Symphony* ("Olympic")
Symphony Orchestra of the National Philharmonic, conducted by Andrzej Markowski. XL 0486

Stanisław Wiechowicz: *Kantata żniwna* (Harvest Cantata)
Choir of the Polish Radio in Cracow, conducted by Alojzy
Kluczniok. L 0055

Stanisław Wisłocki: *Concerto for Piano and Orchestra*
Lidia Grychtołówna (piano), Symphony Orchestra of the National Philharmonic, conducted by Stanisław Wisłocki. XL 0205

V. IN THE VAN OF WORLD MUSIC

"Warsaw Autumn" Festivals; International Contacts and Successes; Activation of Music Life, Competitions, Performers, Ensembles; Leading Composers of 1956—65

The rise in the international stock of contemporary Polish music, which began in 1956 and gained momentum in the years which followed, sprang from the maturing of many individual talents and creative energies combining with social transformations which brought liberalization to all spheres of life and so gave it the room to explore at will. Without the latter, such things as the organization of the 1st International Festival of Contemporary Music in Warsaw, the development of numerous and fruitful international contacts, or the setting up of the Experimental Studio would never have been possible. Nor would the creative adaptation of the latest composing techniques, or the many other phenomena which gave a completely new look to contemporary Polish music and consequently raised it to the position it now occupies.

The cultural policy of the late fifties unchanneled an immense reservoir of initiative leading to the organization of many stimulating events at home and active participation in the main centres of contemporary music abroad. The annual "Warsaw Autumn" Festivals provided a focus for the interests and endeavours of the entire Polish music world. The Fitelberg Composers' Competitions, started in 1958 by the Polish Radio, and the Young Composers' Competitions, launched by the Polish Composers' Union in the same year, offered a great chance to newcomers. The Polish Music Press added its own vigorous contribution to the promotion of Polish music. So, too, did leading orchestras and conductors, especially the National Philharmonic under Witold Rowicki and the Polish Radio Grand Symphony Orchestra under Jan Krenz on the growing number of concert tours for which they were invited. Old contacts with the international music world were revived and new ones established through the International Society for Contemporary Music (SIMC), UNESCO, the International New Music Holiday Courses in Darmstadt, the SIMC festivals, the Venice Biennale, festivals in Donaueschingen, Palermo, Zagreb, etc.

The first visible signs of the transformations in progress were the admission of Poland to the Music Council of UNESCO, and the organization — as the brainchild of Tadeusz Baird and Kazimierz Serocki — of the first of the "Warsaw Autumn" International Festivals of Contemporary Music. Although the programme included the first performances of Serocki's *Sinfonietta* and Baird's *Cassazione,* as well as a wide selection of other Polish works, it was basically a retrospective review of the most interesting achievements of 20th-century music, and a real confrontation of contemporary Polish music with that of other countries only came with the establishment of the "Warsaw Autumn" as an annual review of work in progress with the main accent on Polish composers. This resembled the situation of 1939 when the SIMC Festival, held in Warsaw a few months before the outbreak of World War II, had de-

monstrated that Polish music was climbing to a par
with Europe's other centres of rich and well-estab-
lished traditions.

Some fifteen years later, Witold Lutosławski so described the objectives and achievements of the "Warsaw
Autumn":

> The main purpose of the Festival is to ensure the Polish
> public regular contact with the music of our times... When
> I was a young student of composition, Warsaw was, from
> the point of view of contemporary music, practically a pro-
> vincial town. In contrast to musicians the best of whom
> appeared regularly in Warsaw, the names of modern compo-
> sers were the greatest of rarities. Every young composer
> dreamed therefore of getting abroad and spending some time in
> one of the more lively music centres. It is, for instance... a fact
> as extraordinary as it is sad that Stravinsky's *Rite of Spring*
> was first heard in Poland at the first 'Warsaw Autumn' Fe-
> stival. It took the 'Autumn' to make Warsaw count interna-
> tionally as a centre of contemporary music. (Tadeusz Ka-
> czyński, op. cit., p. 106).

From the outset the "Warsaw Autumn" attracted an
immense audience, now groomed for the reception of
contemporary music by the proselytizing endeavours
of the distinguished conductor, Bohdan Wodiczko, who
from 1955 to 1959 had been in charge of the National
Philharmonic and with such associates as Stanisław
Skrowaczewski had performed the difficult task of ac-
quainting the public, often for the first time, with the
work of composers like Stravinsky, Milhaud, Honegger,
Hindemith, Britten, Orff, Messiaen, Berg and Lieber-
mann.

A large number of young Polish musicians also entered various international music competitions in 1956,
demonstrating that, in spite of the isolation of the preceding years, the standard of performance in Poland

had not fallen below that of other countries. Stanisław Skrowaczewski was awarded 1st prize at the conductors' competition in Rome, Andrzej Czajkowski 3rd prize at the Queen Elisabeth piano competition in Brussels, soprano Halina Łukomska 1st prize in Hertogenbosch, bass Bernard Ładysz 1st prize in Vercelli, and the piano duet of Janina Baster and Janusz Dolny 2nd prize at the same competition. These were only some of the awards, medals and citations won that year.

In 1957 there came a number of important events which laid the foundation for the further development of music life. The aforementioned General Congress of the Polish Composers' Union ushered in a period of intensive clearance of both the domestic and external arrears. A National Committee of the UNESCO International Music Council was formed. The fortnightly Ruch Muzyczny was revived in Cracow, edited by Bronisław Rutkowski and published by the Polish Music Press, and presently became a hive of modern, progressive ideas. In the summer of the same year, a group of young composers (Dobrowolski, Kotoński, Krenz, Markowski, Serocki, Zathey) attended the 12th International New Music Holiday Course in Darmstadt and established a lasting liaison that continued through the years that followed. Soon afterwards, the Polish Society for Contemporary Music was resuscitated as a Section of SIMC. At the end of 1957, the Polish Radio set up its Experimental Studio under Józef Patkowski. Among the many international successes of young musicians, pride of place belongs to Jadwiga Romańska's 1st prize at the singing competition in Munich and Miłosz Magin's 3rd prize at the piano competition in Lisbon. At the Wieniawski Competition on the other hand, Polish violinists made a poorer showing, the top awards going to Rosa Fajn (Soviet Union), and to Sidney Harth (USA) and citations being the best they achieved.

In 1958, the Polish Radio Experimental Studio got into its stride. The 1st Young Composers' Competition brought new names to light (Juliusz Łuciuk, Lucjan Kaszycki, Tadeusz Natanson, Jadwiga Szajna-Lewandowska). A Culture Council was formed as an advisory body to the Minister of Culture and Art, composed of representatives of all the arts, with terms of reference covering the most vital problems of artistic life.

The first performance of Witold Lutosławski's *Musique Funèbre*, and the Fitelberg Composers' Competition, at which the prizes were won by Tadeusz Baird for *Four Essays*, Kazimierz Serocki for *Oczy Powietrza* (Eyes of the Air) and *Musica concertante*, and Włodzimierz Kotoński for *Chamber Music*, showed that the on-going overhaul of vocabulary and awareness was bearing fruit. Grażyna Bacewicz and Witold Lutosławski travelled to Strasbourg as observers at the SIMC Festival. Kazimierz Serocki's *Musica concertante* was included in the programme of the Darmstadt holiday course and Jan Krenz's *Rhapsody* in the Venice Biennale. The 2nd "Warsaw Autumn" Festival — which from then on was to be held every year — brought the first performances of *Symphonic Variations* by Grażyna Bacewicz, the songs *Serce nocy* (The Heart of the Night) by Serocki, *Four Essays* by Baird, *Chamber Music* by Kotoński, and *Epitaph* by the young Henryk Górecki who was the sensation of this and succeeding Festivals. Among those present at the 2nd "Warsaw Autumn" was Karlheinz Stockhausen.

Prizes were again won by Polish singers at competitions in Hertogenbosch (Halina Słonicka, Jerzy Artysz) and Toulouse (Krystyna Szostek-Radkowa), but no less noteworthy was the first major concert tour of the National Philharmonic Orchestra and Choir in Belgium, Federal Republic of Germany and Britain. Its notices gave it a high place in the European hierarchy, an opinion that the tours of 1959 and 1960 served to confirm.

Performances of Polish music abroad and international contacts now grew apace. At the beginning of 1959, Witold Lutosławski became a member of the Jury of the International Society for Contemporary Music (SIMC), then a member of the board of this organization, and eventually, in 1960, its vice-president. In 1959, Polish music won its greatest success to date: UNESCO's Tribune des Compositeurs in Paris awarded first place to Lutosławski's *Musique Funèbre* and Baird's *Four Essays,* and seventh to Serocki's *Sinfonietta*. This resulted in numerous performances abroad of these and other Polish works. At the 2nd Young Composers' Competition the discovery was the remarkable Krzysztof Penderecki whose *Stanzas, Emanations and David's Psalms* collected the first three prizes; Augustyn Bloch's *Espressioni* was awarded a distinction. The Polish Radio Experimental Studio, now in full swing, organized a seminar for composers and theorists, attended by the Italian avant-garde composer Franco Evangelisti. At the Fitelberg Competition, Bogusław Schäffer made his official début as a composer and won an honorary citation for his *Monosonata* and *Quattri movimenti*. In Darmstadt, Włodzimierz Kotoński's *Musique en relief* was given its first performance. The 3rd "Warsaw Autumn", at which Pierre Schaeffer delivered a lecture on experimental music, brought further first performances of new Polish works, among them *Music for Strings, Trumpets and Percussion* by Grażyna Bacewicz, *1st Symphony* by Henryk Górecki and *Improvisation* by Bolesław Szabelski, the latter an eye-opening example of a no longer young composer embracing the new technique. Last but not least, the award of the Prix Italia to Zbigniew Wiszniewski introduced yet another Polish name to the international scene.

Among performers, Hertogenbosch revealed the vocal talent of Zofia Janukowicz, who won the 1st prize, while Halina Słonicka, Jerzy Artysz and Zdzisław Nikodem did well at the singers' competition in Toulouse.

In 1960, the Paris Tribune des Compositeurs awarded its 3rd prize to Grażyna Bacewicz for *Music for Strings, Trumpets and Percussion*. Kotoński's *Musique en relief* was performed at the SIMC Festival in Cologne. Meanwhile, in Poland new names were emerging and the youngest generation consolidating its avantgarde position. The 3rd Young Composers' Competition brought awards to Górecki for *Monologhi I,* Zbigniew Penherski for *Ostinata* and Henryk Schiller for *Music No. 2.* A special competition on the 550th anniversary of the Battle of Grunwald made the name of Romuald Twardowski. In 1960, Wojciech Kilar won the annual prize of the Lili Boulanger Foundation in New York for *Ode Béla Bartók in Memoriam.* At the Fitelberg Competition, prizes were awarded to Serocki for *Episodes,* Penderecki for 8'37" *(Threnody to the Victims of Hiroshima)* and Schäffer for *Equivalenze sonore* and *Topophonica.* The 4th "Warsaw Autumn" was electrified by first performances of works by the young avant-garde: Górecki *(Scontri),* Penderecki *(Dimensions of Time and Silence)* and Schäffer *(Tertium datur).*

The more conventional highlight of music life in

1960 was the 6th International Chopin Competition won by the Italian pianist Maurizio Pollini. Though Polish performers were unplaced they did better elsewhere, Andrzej Jasiński collecting the 1st prize at the piano competition in Barcelona, and Joachim Grubich at the organ competition in Graz. Awards were also won at several singing competitions: Halina Słonicka and Jerzy Artysz (Geneva), Teresa Żylis-Gara and Bożena Lewgowd (Munich), Irena Torbus-Mierzwiakowa (Hertogenbosch), Krystyna Szostek-Radkowa (Vercelli), Hanna Rumowska and Kazimierz Pustelak (Toulouse).

In 1961, the diffusion of contemporary Polish music reached its zenith. Józef Patkowski presented the achievements of the Experimental Studio at a concert in Stockholm and at a congress in Venice. The programme of the Venice Biennale included works by Grażyna Bacewicz, Kotoński, Lutosławski, Łuciuk, Penderecki and Schäffer. The Tribune des Compositeurs in Paris awarded Penderecki's *Threnody*. At the Zagreb Biennale, Lutosławski delivered a lecture on contemporary composing technique, illustrated by Polish examples. Works by Penderecki and Schäffer were performed at the SIMC Festival in Vienna, and the young composer Krystyna Moszumańska-Nazar received a citation for her *Hexaèdre* at a competition in Mannheim. Baird, Górecki, Lutosławski and Penderecki were performed at the International Festival of Contemporary Music in Osaka and Penderecki's *Emanations* and Kotoński's *Canto* in Darmstadt. Finally, Górecki's *1st Symphony* was awarded at the Young Composers' Biennale in Paris. Meanwhile, at the 4th Young Composers' Competition, organized by the Polish Composers' Union, prizes went to Romuald Twardowski for

Antiphones, Stefan Behr for *Piece in 5 Movements,* Leoncjusz Ciuciura for *Canti al fresco,* and Zbigniew Bujarski for *Zones.* The Fitelberg Competition brought citations to Stefan Behr for *Epitaphe* and to Józef Świder for *Concertino.* The programme of the 5th "Warsaw Autumn" comprised a large number of first performances, including *Jeux Vénitiens* by Lutosławski, *Poems* by Szabelski, *Pensieri notturni* by Bacewicz, *Herbsttag* by Kilar, and *Erotiques* by Baird.

The same year also ushered in a considerable enlivenment of musical theatre. The imminent opening of the rebuilt Grand Theatre in Warsaw prompted certain radical measures. Until then, the Warsaw Opera, hampered in any case by the very difficult conditions in its temporary premises, only sporadically took on some more challenging enterprise. A conventional repertoire, traditional and lack-lustre staging, a mediocre company, had left it outshone by the other attractions of music life. In 1961, the energetic and talented Bohdan Wodiczko was appointed manager, and a stream of new productions soon followed, works never before attempted were presented, the services of the best stage designers engaged, foreign ballet masters and directors invited. Within a single season, the Opera captured the interest of the entire music and theatre-going public and became one of the highlights of the artistic scene.

In 1962 the international prominence of contemporary Polish music, especially of its two leading representatives, Lutosławski and Penderecki, was further entrenched. Penderecki's *Polymorphia* was performed in Hamburg, his *String Quartet* (by the LaSalle Quartet) in Cincinnati, and *Fluorescences* in Donaueschingen; the bill at the Venice Biennale included his *Threnody,* together with Górecki's *Scontri* and Kotoński's *Pezzo per flauto e pianoforte*. At the Malawski Composers' Competition in Cracow, Penderecki's *Canon* took the 1st prize, the 2nd and 3rd going to Schäffer (for *Musica ipsa*) and Schiller (for *Inventions*). Finally, among the winners of the newly established awards of the Minister of Culture and Art were Penderecki (for *Threnody*) and Lutosławski (for the whole of his work). Others were: Wiechowicz (for *Letter to Marc Chagall*), Baird (for *Four Essays*), Szabelski (for *Sonnets, Improvisations* and *Poems*) and Bacewicz (for *Pensieri notturni*).

These honours were one more token of the official recognition extended to the avant-garde and a sign that the old aesthetic dogmas had been replaced by sober assessment of facts. In the summer of that year, Lutosławski visited the American music centre in Tanglewood to deliver a series of lectures, while his *Jeux Vénitiens* was a great success at the Tribune des Compositeurs in Paris. The stock of other Polish composers continued to soar: Bairds' *Erotiques* and Kotoński's *Trio* were performed at the SIMC Festival in London. Electronic music by Dobrowolski and Wiszniewski was presented at concerts in Stockholm and Cologne (the Experimental Studio received one of the Polish Radio's annual awards for achievements to date). Young composers, Łuciuk, Ciuciura and Moszumańska-Nazar, scored at competitions in Utrecht, Prague and Buenos Aires. The 6th "Warsaw Autumn" brought several first performances of new Polish works, and the Young Composers' Competition marked the discovery among the youngest generation: Zbigniew Rudziński, Bogusław Pasternak, Jerzy Maksymiuk and Tomasz Sikorski.

It was also a very good year for young Polish performers. At the Casella Piano Competition in Naples,

Jerzy Gajek was awarded 2nd prize. Splendid triumphs were recorded by Delfina Ambroziak (1st prize at the singing competition in Munich), Joachim Grubich (1st prize at the organ competition in Geneva), and Zofia Wilma (2nd prize at the singing competition in Hertogenbosch). At the music competition which accompanied the Youth Festival in Helsinki, Aleksander Migdał (violin) and Tadeusz Prochowski (singing) won 1st prizes and Jerzy Gonczorowski (trumpet) a 2nd prize. Elsewhere successes in international competitions were scored by Roman Siwek (trombone), Marta Sosińska (piano), Teresa May (singing), Wiesław Ochman (singing), and many others. The Wieniawski Violin Competition in Poznań attracted a somewhat weaker entry than usual, the first three places being taken by Charles Treger (USA), Oleg Krysa (USSR) and Krzysztof Jakowicz (Poland).

The most notable features of 1963, apart from many performances of Polish works abroad, were four outstanding international achievements: Tadeusz Baird received the annual Music Award of the City of Cologne, the Rainier III Composers' Competition in Monaco awarded prizes to Witold Rudziński for the opera *Odprawa posłów greckich* (Dismissal of the Greek Envoys), and to Augustyn Bloch for the ballet *Expectation*, the Tribune des Compositeurs singled out Baird's *Variations without Theme* and Twardowski's *Antiphones* and, finally, Witold Lutosławski was elected to the Swedish Royal Academy of Music and soon afterwards won the 1st award at a competition organized in Vienna by the Gesellschaft der Musikfreunde and UNESCO.

Other events worth noting were, in addition to the "Warsaw Autumn", the 1963 awards of the Minister of

Culture and Art presented to Kazimierz Serocki for the whole of his work and to Witold Rudziński for contributions to opera; a three-month tour of the Soviet Union, Japan and Australia by the Polish Radio Grand Symphony Orchestra under Jan Krenz; and successes by Polish singers at annual competitions abroad: Ewa Dąbrowska (Hertogenbosch, 2nd prize), Antoni Dutkiewicz (Hertogenbosch, 2nd prize), Andrzej Saciuk (Munich, 2nd prize), Henryk Grychnik (Geneva, 2nd prize), Magdalena Bojanowska (Vienna, 3rd prize) and Hanna Rejmer (Liège, 2nd prize).

In 1964 came further successes for Witold Lutosławski: the Koussevitzky International Award for *Trois Poèmes d'Henri Michaux*, which also won honours at the Tribune des Compositeurs in Paris. He was in addition the recipient of a State Award Class I.

Of the many international contacts mention should be made of the growing exchange with Japan, begun a year earlier by performances of Lutosławski and Penderecki at the 1st International Festival of Contemporary Music in Osaka. A rare tribute was paid at the SIMC Festival in Copenhagen by the inclusion of four Polish works (by Baird, Serocki, Górecki and Szalonek) instead of the customary two. A considerable amount of Polish music was also presented at the Venice Biennale. The Fitelberg Competition brought awards to Zbigniew Bujarski, Zbigniew Penherski and Bogusław Schäffer; the Young Composers' Competition spotlighted the names of Jan Astriab, Zbigniew Ciechan and Zenon Kowalowski.

Among performers, the greatest achievement was the 1st and 2nd awards at the competition in Hertogenbosch won by singers Bożena Kinasz-Mikołajczak and Anna Malewicz.

The annual award of the Polish Composers' Union for 1965 went to Kazimierz Serocki. At the Rainier III Competition in Monaco, the 3rd prize was awarded to Romuald Twardowski for his ballet *The Sorcerer's Statues*. At the "Harmonien" Music Society's competition in Bergen, Witold Rudziński won the 1st prize for his *Pictures from the Świętokrzyskie Mountains* for orchestra. Grażyna Bacewicz received the Award of the Belgian Government and the Gold Medal at the Queen Elisabeth Composers' Competition for her *7th Violin Concerto*. Augustyn Bloch's ballet *The Bull* was acclaimed at the Holland Festival. Works by other Polish composers did well at the Festival in Madrid, and in Athens and Stockholm. The "Warsaw Autumn" produced a large amount of new music.

In Poland the outstanding event was the 7th Chopin Piano Competition at which the prize-winners were (in descending order): Martha Argerich (Argentina), Arthur Moreira-Lima (Brazil), Marta Sosińska (Poland), Hiroko Nakamura (Japan), Edward Auer (USA) and Elżbieta Głąb (Poland).

Another highlight was the opening, after many years of reconstruction, of the Grand Theatre in Warsaw which with productions of Moniuszko's *The Haunted Manor* and *Halka*, Różycki's *Pan Twardowski* and Szymanowski's *King Roger* launched a new era in the history of Warsaw Opera.

Among the successes scored by young artists at competitions abroad, Kazimierz Myrlak won a 1st prize in Toulouse (singing), Teresa Wojtaszek-Kubiak a 2nd prize in Munich (singing), Elżbieta Stefańska-Łukowicz a 2nd prize in Geneva (harpsichord) and Teresa May a 2nd prize in Budapest (singing).

This summary review of the main international triumphs of contemporary Polish music in 1956—65 offers unmistakable evidence that contemporary music in Poland had attained a level and impetus it had never known before. What was particularly encouraging was that it owed its rise not to a few talented individuals but to a very large body of composers of different generations, the most numerous furthermore being the youngest, which was a guarantee that it would add to its laurels. Some foreign observers found it legitimate to talk of a lasting contribution to the development of contemporary music, resulting in a realignment of the traditional structure of Europe's avant-garde. A revealing re-evaluation hits the eye when comparing works on contemporary music written by west European authors before 1965 with more recent publications: in the former Polish music occupies only a token place, if that; in the latter it has whole chapters devoted to it.

The composer most looked up to in this period was Witold Lutosławski, each new work of his hailed as a landmark: *Five Songs* for voice and chamber orchestra (1956—58), *Musique Funèbre* for string orchestra (1958), *Jeux Vénitiens* for symphony orchestra (1961), *Trois Poèmes d'Henri Michaux* for choir and orchestra (1962—63), *String Quartet* (1964) and *Paroles tissées* for tenor and orchestra (1965). Written with great deliberation and a sense of classical perfection, studiously worked out to the most minute detail, they all represent an individual, independent style in which inventiveness blends with formal and technical discipline into an integral whole. Not that Lutosławski repeats himself; the same masterly proficiency is brought to bear on some new creative problem. In *Five Songs,* he explored the potential of a harmony free of the limitations of tonal thinking and the expressive and colour possibilities of the twelve-note scale. Abandonment of the tonal system did not, however, mean surrendering to the constraints of dodecaphonist or any other rules, but a search for his own system of organization of sound. The long-maturing *Musique Funèbre* was the first product of this painstakingly developed original vocabulary. *Jeux Vénitiens* marked a dip into the aleatory idiom, enlarged upon in *String Quartet* and *Trois Poèmes*, which are dazzlingly colourful into the bargain. Here we have a personal variation on the technique known as "controlled aleatorism", consisting, to quote Lutosławski's own description, "in a use of the element of chance which enriches the rhythm and expression of the music, without in the least loosening the composer's complete grip on its final shape". For Lutosławski, recourse to the latest techniques has never been an aim in itself. He is one of the few composers who can digest them into music which is relatively easy listening, has an intelligible logic of form, and abounds in expressiveness.

Of his juniors, the composer who made the most forceful impression was Tadeusz Baird who hammered out an original style of his own relatively early in his career. In contrast to Lutosławski whose explorations owe nothing to the Vienna school, he represents, both in technique and in expression, one of its creative offshoots. Such interests were already intimated in *Cassazione* (1956) and continued in *String Quartet* (1957), *Four Essays* for orchestra (1958), *Espressioni* for violin and orchestra (1959), *Homily* for reciting voice, choir and orchestra (1960), *Erotiques* for soprano and orchestra 1961), *Variations without Theme* for orchestra

(1962), *Epiphany Music* for symphony orchestra (1963) and *Four Dialogues* for oboe and chamber orchestra (1964). This fairly prolific output is by no means of a piece. Though predominantly — and typically — reflective and lyrical, it also contains its more sonorous moments *(Homily)*, and echoes of Szymanowski *(Espressioni)*. The treatment of form and sound organization is equally varied: next to tight-knit twelve-tone structures we have essays in pointillisme and even a complete subordination of form to lyrical invention *(Epiphany Music)*. Nevertheless the individuality of his music and the independence of his imagination have a strength which gives all this diversity the common stamp of a distinctive type of emotion, a subtle sense of colour, expressive melody and, above all, a supremacy of feeling over construction.

In a vignette of Baird, "Poland's most significant musical lyricist since Szymanowski", the distinguished music critic, Karl H. Wörner wrote in the American journal, the Musical Quarterly (1962):

His first international success was achieved by his *Four Essays* for orchestra... Here a modern composer is writing modern beautiful music, without a dubious or inferior aspect being in the least associated with the word 'beautiful'. Much is reminiscent of Alban Berg, but everything is simpler, more transparent, smoother, more homophonic — yet, despite all naturalness, most highly refined in artistic sensibility. His great melodic inspiration makes available to him wide, concentrated tensions within the framework of the twelve-tone technique. It is an expressive type of music, which now and then pushes on into the heights of the ecstatic — Alban Berg reborn and rejuvenated in the Slavic world.

For Kazimierz Serocki the organization of sound was a problem of much greater interest, each new work probing the possibilities of the contemporary idioms. He was one of the first Polish composers to be drawn to the twelve-tone technique and followed up his early efforts in two cycles of songs for voice and piano: *The Heart of the Night* (1956) and *The Eyes of the Air* (1957), re-arranged for voice and chamber orchestra in 1960. *Musica concertante* for orchestra (1958) marked a first attempt at total serialization, with all the elements of the music embraced by note-row. The same technique was used in *Episodes* for strings and three groups of percussion instruments, but now combined with interesting experiments in space effects. With *Segments* for chamber orchestra (1961) he produced an interesting blend of musique concrète with his previous methods of organizing the sound material. In *A piacere — Proposals for Piano* (1963), he tapped the aleatoric method. Finally, in the powerful *Symphonic Frescoes* for orchestra (1963) came a synthesis of these persevering, wide-ranging explorations and experiments and their transplantation to a piece of symphonic scale, which also outlined a new and arresting musical architecture.

Among the very oldest generation the most striking figure continued to be Bolesław Szabelski who swallowed the new musical vocabulary in his stride, an evolution which surprised many, though not closer observers of his work, who found the basic feature of his style unchanged. The last work of his preceding neo-Baroque period was the *4th Symphony* (1958), austere and moderate in its modernness. In 1959, Szabelski produced *Improvisations* for mixed choir and chamber orchestra, in which he used twelve-tone technique, thereby confounding his stabilized, somewhat conservative reputation. As it turned out later, he had already a year earlier composed the pointilliste *Sonnets* for orchestra (1958). His subsequent works: *Poems* for piano and chamber orchestra (1959), *Aphorisms 9* for ten performers (1962), *Preludes* for chamber orchestra (1963) and *Concerto for Flute and Chamber Orchestra* (1965), demonstrated that his interest in the new music was of a lasting nature. Use of twelve-tone technique did not, however, mean submitting rigorously to its principles. His music, dramatic and full of contrasts, has a clear structure and a logic of its own springing from an innate sense of form rather than the characteristics of the technique.

Włodzimierz Kotoński, Andrzej Dobrowolski and Zbigniew Wiszniewski formed a group deeply excited by the possibilities of experimental music.

Kotoński, the author of Percussion Instruments in the Modern Orchestra, published in 1963, had undergone an enormous evolution: from interest in highland folklore to avant-garde composing techniques. This new period began with the pointilliste *Chamber Music* for 21 instruments and percussion (1958). Then came *Muique en relief* for orchestra (1959), which made use of space effects, *Trio* for flute, guitar and percussion (1960) with elements of aleatorism, and *Canto* for chamber orchestra (1961). Logical extensions of his exploration of rhythm and sound were *Selection I* for four jazz musicians (1962), *Musica per fiati e timpani* (1963), and *Quintet* for wind instruments (1964). He also had two pieces of musique concrète for recording tape to his name: *Etude concrète* (1959) and *Microstructures* (1963).

Andrzej Dobrowolski followed a similar path, the twelve-tone *Studies* for oboe, trumpet, bassoon and double-bass (1959), *Symphony Concertante* for oboe, clarinet, bassoon and string orchestra (1960) and *Music for Strings and Four Groups of Wind Instruments* (1964), being accompanied by electronic music: *Passacaglia* (1959), *Music for Recording Tape No. 1* (1962) and *Music for Recording Tape and Solo Oboe* (1965).

Zbigniew Wiszniewski (b. 1922) made his début as a composer much later and immediately turned to the new techniques. The results included a radio opera *Neffru* (1959), *Concetrazioni espressive* for chamber ensemble (1960), the ballet *Ad hominem* (1962), *Three Electronic Postludes* (1962), *Sonata for Solo Violin* (1963), *Trio* for oboe, harp and viola (1963), and *Tre pezzi della tradizione* (1964).

Among composers of a more moderate bent pride of place belongs, by virtue of her international reputation and creative achievements, to Grażyna Bacewicz. Her output in the period under discussion included *Symphonic Variations* (1957), *Music for Strings, Trumpets and Percussion* (1958), the radio opera *Adventures of King Arthur* (1959), *Pensieri notturni* for 24 instruments (1961), *Concerto for Orchestra* (1962), *2nd Cello Concerto* (1963) and *Musica sinfonica in tre movimenti* (1965). These works indicate a marked evolution towards deeper expression and more radical language, without, however, any sacrifice of her individual style.

The temptation of note-row technique, distinctively interpreted, also overtook Zygmunt Mycielski in his *2nd Symphony* (1960), awarded a prize at the Competition in Monaco. The tight organization of the whole flow of this interesting piece was intended to be a kind of protest against the use of the chance element in art.

Two arresting impressive works came from Stanisław Wiechowicz: *Letter to Marc Chagall* (1961), a dramatic rhapsody for solo voices, choir and orchestra, and *The Dove* (1963), a cantata.

Kazimierz Sikorski, continuing his construction of a solo repertoire for wind instruments, wrote concertos for flute (1957), trumpet (1960) and bassoon (1965), masterly works with a distinctly Polish flavour.

Tadeusz Szeligowski, true to his chosen bearings, composed, among others, *Psalm* for boys' choir *a capella* (1960), an oratorio *Odysseus Weeping* (1961), a cantata, *Rex gloriosus* (1962), and an unfinished opera *Gentleman Theodore*.

Witold Rudziński wrote a number of interesingly-conceived works, including the opera *The Commandant of Paris* (1959), *Deux portraits des femmes* for soprano and string quartet (1960), *The Roof of the World* for reciting voice and orchestra (1960), *Musique Concertante* for piano and orchestra (1961), the opera *Dismissal of the Greek Envoys* (1963), which is of particular merit and awarded at Monaco, *Pictures from the Świętokrzyskie Mountains* for orchestra, and an oratorio, *Gaude Mater Polonia*. This composer walks somewhat alone in contemporary Polish music. In an interview published in Ruch Muzyczny (No. 1, 1972), he stated:

Among the various currents and styles in contemporary music, I am interested in one which is now the least orthodox, a certain type of programme music. It has even become the fashion to regard it as 'not done' to speak of such things. When I wrote *Pictures from the Świętokrzyskie Mountains,* I remarked to a musician that its programme was a poetic commentary to the lyrical scenes from Żeromski's *Ashes.* Not only was he most upset, but he warned me to be careful not to say anything of this sort in public, because it might give me a bad name. Perhaps it does reflect badly on me, but at least I am following in quite a respectable tradition, Liszt, Couperin, Karłowicz, Richard Strauss to look no further. The plain fact of the matter is that programme music is legitimate and cold-shouldering it is no proof of being modern. In any case, many of the contemporary composers who profess to have no time for programme music are in effect writing it, and very good it often is.

The work of composers like Kisielewski, Turski, Woytowicz, Perkowski and such, on the other hand, took a back seat, the last of these being the arch-conservative. Not that the new wave had, despite appearances, gripped the whole music world, although the general atmosphere, the sympathies of the critics, and even a certain degree of prejudice in favour of experiment generated a psychological climate complained of as avant-garde "terror". Opposed to, or unaffected by it, remained quite a numerous group of composers of various generations (Ryszard Bukowski, Edward Bury, Florian Dąbrowski, Maria Dziewulska, Irena Garztecka, Czesław Grudziński, Henryk Jabłoński, Tomasz Kiesewetter, Tadeusz Machl, Krzysztof A. Mazur, Jerzy Młodziejowski, Karol Mroszczyk, Tadeusz Paciorkiewicz, Konrad Pałubicki, Stefan B. Poradowski, Jadwiga Szajna-Lewandowska, Władysław Walentynowicz, Kazimierz Wiłkomirski, and others), active for the most part outside Warsaw, and represented at such regional festivals as the "Opole Spring", the "Poznań Spring", the Festival of Western Territories Composers, etc. Although some of these names are well worth noting, their achievements made little more than local impact.

What did emerge in these years, however, was a large group of newcomers wedded to the extreme avant-garde. The most original was unquestionably Krzysztof Penderecki (b. 1933) who, within years, built up an international reputation to become Poland's best-known composer after Lutosławski. His output was prolific: *Epitaph* for string orchestra and kettle-drums (1958), *David's Psalms* for mixed choir and percussion (1958), *Emanations* for two string bands (1958), *Stanzas* for soprano, reciting voice and ten instruments (1959), *Anaclasis* for strings and percussion (1960), *Threnody for the Victims of Hiroshima (8'37")* for 52 string instruments, *String Quartet* (1960), *Psalmus 1961* — electronic music (1961), *Polymorphia* for string instruments (1962), *Stabat Mater* for choir *a cappella* (1962), *Fluorescences* for symphony orchestra, *Sonata* for cello and orchestra (1964), *Capriccio* for oboe and strings (1965) and, finally, the masterpiece of this period, the monumental *St. Luke Passion* (1965). The most exciting feature of his music was probably the exploration of new sound qualities, beginning with *Anaclasis* its most arresting characteristic. Abandoning specified pitch, intervals, melodic line, etc, he was bent on arriving at colour composition extracted by means of new methods of articulation, the principal field of experiment being the new possibilities of strings — it is the skilful handling of sound sequences and dynamic contrasts which makes Penderecki's music so dramatic to listen to. With the *Passion,* however, he proved himself more than an avant-garde seeker after novelty. All his previous experiments were here superbly justified in the working out of one of those overriding creative ideas that have inspired European art from its beginnings. Penderecki's world of sounds, so startling at a first hearing, will seem less exotic in the context of the following statement:

The emancipation of sound colour as an equal element of the composition has a long tradition behind it. Listen to any of Tchaikovsky's symphonies, forgetting their harmonic evo-

lution and the specific pitch of the various sounds, and con-
centrating only on the development of the instrumental sound,
its colour, dynamics, register, the duration of each sound, its
density and width in terms of the whole score, the kinds of
figuration in the strings, etc. You will find that the evolution
is extremely interesting in itself, rich and absolutely controlled.
In artistic value, it sometimes considerably surpasses the harmonic content of the work — just compare it with the piano
score. With Tchaikovsky, these things are, of course, still strictly
connected with one another, and listening to him in the way
I have proposed is an artificial experiment. It brings home,
however, that a habit of responding to the sound of music
took root a long time ago — although at first strictly in an
interval context. It can also be clearly seen that the hegemony of this factor has been increasing and at times became absolutely predominant. Take, for instance, the magnificent ending
of the *Pathétique* with its gradual muting of the strings, down
to cellos and double-basses in *pppp*. The choice of intervals is
insignificant here, the important thing is the very effect of the
softness of the strings gradually dissolving into a murmur.
...To me as a composer, this element of the composition, enriched with new sounds by new means of articulation, is what
matters most. (Interview for *Nutida Musik,* No. 1, 1963—64).

In this same interview, Penderecki, the leading representative of the young Polish avant-garde in the
sixties, spelled out his attitude towards tradition:

Is it in practice possible to cut onself off from the whole
history of music or to create a system of new laws without
tapping the achievements of earlier periods? Can there be
a generation with that immense a creative potential, however
much it may have been dreamed of by each of them from
Romanticism on. The revolution always proves incomplete because we bear too heavy a load of habits which make themselves felt even in our boldest explorations. Contemporary
audiences often fondly imagine they are witnessing something
totally transformed and draw an artificial distinction between
the heretofore, or traditional, and the new, supposedly wholly

unlike it. ...It is only the vocabulary that changes in music — the sound material and its grammar — but the general principles of consistency of style, logic and economy of development, authenticity of experience, remain the same. Good music is a concept which still means exactly what it used to.

Wojciech Kilar (b. 1932), who had made his début before Penderecki, now progressed from those early pieces. In *Ode Béla Bartók in Memoriam* (1957), *Concerto for Two Pianos and Percussion* (1958), *Herbsttag* for soprano and string quartet (1960), *Riff 62* for orchestra (1962), *Génerique* for orchestra (1963), *Diphthonyos* for choir and orchestra (1964) and *Springfield Sonnet* for orchestra (1965) he underwent a striking evolution from the influence of Bartók to the poetic atmosphere of Webern-like pointillisme and eventually work of a fully original nature, remarkable for its economy, simplicity of construction, sharpness of sound, ebullience and powerful feeling.

A very interesting figure among the young musical avant-garde was Bogusław Schäffer (b. 1929), a distinguished theorist of the new music with numerous publications to his name. At first he kept his composing *sub rosa* and did not have it performed in public until 1959. His major works are: *Quattro movimenti* for piano and orchestra (1958), *Tertium datur,* a composer's treatise for harpsichord and instruments (1958), *Monosonata* for 24 string instruments (1959), *Scultura* for orchestra (1960), *Codes* for chamber orchestra (1961), *Musica ipsa* for orchestra (1961), *S'alto* for saxophone and chamber orchestra (1962), *TIS-MW2: A Stage Composition* (1963), *PR I—V* for cast of actors (1964), *Quartet* for two pianists and any other two performers (1965). Arrestingly original in conception and inventive in structure these pieces are a positive digest of contemporary composing concerns. The most notable feature were perhaps the wholly neoteric notational proposals. But there was also the introduction of the idea of instrumental theatre — and in an interpretation all his own. Nevertheless his music was of a highly cerebral nature and bit off formally more than it could chew in expression.

Henryk Mikołaj Górecki (b. 1933) is Schäffer's opposite, employing a wide variety of techniques, including aleatorism, and possessing an imagination in which expression decidedly prevails over speculation. This was revealed with particular force in *Scontri* for orchestra (1960) where new means were used to achieve a very high degree of emotional tension. His most notable works from this period are: *Songs of Joy and Rhythm* for instrumental ensemble (1957), *Concerto for Five Instruments and a String Quartet* (1957), *Epitaph* for choir and instrumental ensemble (1958), *Symphony 1959* for string orchestra and percussion, *Monologhi* for orchestra (1960), *Genesis* (1963), *Choros I* for string ensemble (1964) and *Refrain* for orchestra (1965). In 1962, in a conversation with his musicologist friend Leon Markiewicz, Górecki said:

If percussion or 'murmur' sounds are being used to a greater extent today, that is the normal evolution of music. It is simply a matter of a different way of organizing and using the entire sound scale. Another point is that today's realities — mechanizations, the wonders of electronics, the huge conglomerations of people — make us perceive things that used to go unobserved. Have you noticed how magnificent a sound phenomenon is a sports stadium filled with a hundred thousand spectators? The jubilant roar of a hundred thousand throats? Their indrawn breath of disappointment? The ebb and flow of excitement governed by the movement of a ball which is so tiny compared to the huge mass of sound? It just can't leave you cold. After all, music is not only the F sharp-A-B flat, but to use Debussy's words, the rustle of the forest and the murmur of water'... Only matters of technique can be discussed in concrete terms, other things are too elusive for words, which is probably why they are expressed through music. It has become a particularly popular belief in the 20th century that the idea, its development, their relation to the unfolding of the musical material, etc. are all that count. But is this really so? Take, for example, Stravinsky, the main exponent of the cult of métier. Why was it he could not dispense with stage music, with an emotionally charged text? Why did he not even once use syllables instead of words?... To me, art is a manifestation of life and I try to convey this manifestation by every means available. Some people rest content in effect with the domain of technique. But perhaps they are the poorer for that part of the mystery of music which makes it an art? (Ruch Muzyczny, No 17, 1962).

In this period the creative personae of most other composers were still in the making. Chief among those already claiming attention was Augustyn Bloch (b. 1929), with such works as the excellent *Espressioni* for soprano and orchestra (1959), *Meditations* for soprano, organ and percussion (1961), *Dialogues* for violin and orchestra (1964) and the ballets, *Voci* (1962), *Expectation* (1963) and *The Bull* (1965). Others to develop in an original way were Witold Szalonek (b. 1927), author of *Confessions* for reciting voice, choir and chamber orchestra (1959), *Concertina* for flute and chamber orchestra (1962) and *Les sons* for symphony orchestra (1965), Juliusz Łuciuk (b. 1927), who made interesting experiments in transforming the traditional sound of the piano (prepared piano), Krystyna Moszumańska-Nazar and Romuald Twardowski (b. 1930).

An exceptionally large number of newcomers arrived on the scene in 1956—65, displaying a thorough knowledge of contemporary composing problems and in most cases an interest in avant-garde explorations: Jerzy Badurski, Stefan Behr, Zbigniew Bujarski, Leoncjusz Ciuciura, Lucjan Kaszycki, Zygmunt Krauze, Jerzy Maksymiuk, Tadeusz Natanson, Bogumił Pasternak, Zbigniew Penherski, Kazimierz Rozbicki, Zbigniew Rudziński, Henryk Schiller, Tomasz Sikorski, Władysław Słowiński, Antoni Szeligowski, Zdzisław Szostak, Józef Świder, Leszek Wisłocki, and others. Some of them were soon to advance into the forefront of Polish music.

The revival of modern music and the re-invigoration of music life in the years 1956—65 were matched in the field of musicology. After a period of stagnation caused by a shortage of staff and by a certain methodological crisis, the early sixties saw it rallying vigorously, much of the momentum coming from young scholars of postwar vintage: Krzysztof Biegański, Michał Bristiger, Andrzej Chodkowski, Anna Czekanowska, Elżbieta Dziębowska, Władysław Malinowski, Jerzy Morawski, Mirosław Perz, Jan Stęszewski and Zygmunt M. Szweykowski. It is true that a concentration of personnel in the Institute of Musicology at Warsaw University (established in 1958), headed by Professor Zofia Lissa, and the Institute of the History and Theory of Polish Music at the Polish Academy of Sciences under Professor Józef M. Chomiński and, after him, Dr Stefan Jarociński, resulted in other centres well-nigh ceasing to exist. Against this it had the advantage of making it possible to undertake several extremely valuable projects.

In 1957, on the initiative of Professor Zofia Lissa, a special Centre for the Documentation and Inventarization of Musical Antiquities in Poland was formed at the Institute of Musicology. Headed by the late Professor Hieronim Feicht, it went to work on a large scale and to remarkably fruitful effect. A number of unknown works were discovered which radically changed the established history of Polish music — above all in the Middle Ages and the Renaissance — and filled in many of the gaps in other periods. Another field of intensive research which yielded numerous publications was Chopin and Szymanowski.

These findings were presented at international musicological congresses organized in Poland in 1960 and 1966. At the same time, the Polish contribution to international scholarship was greatly intensified through conference attendance and participation in the proceedings of various organizations. Numerous publications — notably, Professor Zofia Lissa's works on the aesthetics of music — were translated into foreign languages. It was also from the ranks of musicology graduates that there emerged almost the whole contemporary generation of critics, most of them associated with the fortnightly Ruch Muzyczny, published in Warsaw since 1960 (Ludwik Erhardt, Tadeusz Kaczyński, Józef Kański, Władysław Malinowski, Bohdan Pociej, Jan Weber, Tadeusz A. Zieliński).

RECORDINGS BY "POLSKIE NAGRANIA — MUZA" OF
POLISH MUSIC FROM THE YEARS 1956—65 (selection)

Grażyna Bacewicz: *Music for Strings, Trumpets and Percussion*
  Symphony Orchestra of the National Philharmonic, conducted
  by Witold Rowicki. XL 0171

Grażyna Bacewicz: *Musica sinfonica in tre movimenti; Pensieri notturni*
  Symphony Orchestra of the National Philharmonic, conducted
  by Witold Rowicki. XL 0274

Tadeusz Baird: *Four Essays*
  Symphony Orchestra of the National Philharmonic, conducted
  by Witold Rowicki. XL 0274

Tadeusz Baird: *Espressioni* for violin and orchestra; *Homily*
for reciting voice, choir and orchestra; *Erotiques* for soprano
and orchestra; *Variations without Theme* for orchestra
  Wanda Wiłkomirska (violin), Aleksander Bardini (recitation),
  Stefania Woytowicz (soprano), Symphony Orchestra of the
  National Philharmonic, conducted by Witold Rowicki. XL
  0177

Tadeusz Baird: *Four Dialogues* for oboe and orchestra
  Lothar Faber (oboe), Symphony Orchestra of the National
  Philharmonic, conducted by Witold Rowicki. XL 0336

Tadeusz Baird: *Trouvéres' Songs* for mezzo-soprano, two flutes and cello; *Epiphany Music* for orchestra
  Krystyna Szostek-Radkowa (mezzo-soprano), Symphony Orchestra of the National Philharmonic, conducted by Witold
  Rowicki. XL 0462

Tadeusz Baird: *Shakespeare's Four Love Sonnets* for baritone
and orchestra
  Jerzy Artysz (baritone), Chamber Orchestra of the National
  Philharmonic, conducted by Karol Teutsch. XL 0586

Augustyn Bloch: *Meditations* for soprano, organ and percussion; *Espressioni* for soprano and orchestra

Halina Łukomska (soprano), Symphony Orchestra of the National Philharmonic, conducted by Andrzej Markowski. XL 0394

Edward Bogusławski: *Apocalypsis* for reciting voice, choir and orchestra
Aleksander Bardini (recitation), Choir and Orchestra of the National Philharmonic, conducted by Witold Rowicki. XL 0336

Andrzej Dobrowolski: *Music for Strings and Four Groups of Wind Instruments*
Symphony Orchestra of the National Philharmonic, conducted by Witold Rowicki. XL 0336

Henryk Mikołaj Górecki: *Epitaph; Scontri; Canti strumentali; Refrain*
Polish Radio Grand Symphony Orchestra, conducted by Jan Krenz. XL 0391

Henryk Mikołaj Górecki: *Three Pieces in the Old Style*
Chamber Orchestra of the National Philharmonic, conducted by Karol Teutsch. XL 0586

Wojciech Kilar: *Riff 62* for orchestra
Symphony Orchestra of the National Philharmonic, conducted by Andrzej Markowski. XL 0486

Włodzimierz Kotoński: *Musica per fiati e timpani*
Symphony Orchestra of the National Philharmonic, conducted by Witold Rowicki. XL 0336

Witold Lutosławski: *Musique Funèbre*
Symphony Orchestra of the National Philharmonic, conducted by Witold Rowicki. XL 0072

Witold Lutosławski: *Jeux Vénitiens*
Symphony Orchestra of the National Philharmonic, conducted by Witold Rowicki. XL 0132

Witold Lutosławski: *Trois Poèms d'Henri Michaux* for choir and orchestra; *Postlude*
Choir of the Polish Radio in Cracow, Polish Radio Grand Symphony Orchestra, conducted by Jan Krenz and Witold Lutosławski. XL 0237

Witold Lutosławski: *String Quartet*
LaSalle String Quartet. XL 0282

Witold Lutosławski: *Five Songs* for voice and orchestra
Halina Łukomska (soprano), Symphony Orchestra of the National Philharmonic, conducted by Andrzej Markowski. XL 0394

Witold Lutosławski: *Paroles tissées*
Louis Devos (tenor), Symphony Orchestra of the National Philharmonic, conducted by Witold Lutosławski. XL 0453

Krzysztof Penderecki: *Threnody for the Victims of Hiroshima*
Symphony Orchestra of the National Philharmonic, conducted by Witold Rowicki. XL 0171

Krzysztof Penderecki: *David's Psalms; Sonata per cello e orchestra; Anaclasis; Stabat Mater; Fluorescences*
Choir and Symphony Orchestra of the National Philharmonic, conducted by Andrzej Markowski. XL 0260

Krzysztof Penderecki: *String Quartet*
LaSalle String Quartet: XL 0282

Krzysztof Penderecki: *St. Luke Passion*
Soloists, Choir and Orchestra of the Cracow Philharmonic, conducted by Henryk Czyż. XL 0325—0326

Krzysztof Penderecki: *Polymorphia*
Orchestra of the Cracow Philharmonic, conducted by Henryk Czyż. XL 0413

Witold Rudziński: *Dismissal of the Greek Envoys,* opera in one act
Soloists, Choir and Orchestra of the Grand Theatre in Warsaw, conducted by Antoni Wicherek. XL 0292

Witold Rudziński: *Gaude Mater Polonia*
Soloists, Polish Radio Grand Symphony Orchestra, conducted by Jan Krenz. XL 0454

Witold Rudziński: *The Roof of the World; Pictures from the Świętokrzyskie Mountains*
Wojciech Siemion (recitation), Orchestra of the Grand Theatre in Warsaw, conducted by Antoni Wicherek. XL 0615

Bogusław Schäffer: *Quartet 2+2*
The "Musical Workshop" Ensemble. XL 0573

Kazimierz Serocki: *Sinfonietta* for two string orchestras
Symphony Orchestra of the National Philharmonic, conducted by Witold Rowicki. XL 0072

Kazimierz Serocki: *Musica concertante; Segmenti; Episodes;
Symphonic Frescoes*
Polish Radio Grand Symphony Orchestra, conducted by Jan
Krenz. XL 0267

Kazimierz Serocki: *Eyes of the Air,* a cycle of songs
Halina Łukomska (soprano), Symphony Orchestra of the
National Philharmonic, conducted by Andrzej Markowski.
XL 0394

Tomasz Sikorski: *Concerto breve* for piano, 24 wind instruments and 4 percussions
Tomasz Sikorski (piano), Symphony Orchestra of the National Philharmonic, conducted by Andrzej Markowski. XL 0486

Bolesław Szabelski: *Aphorisms 9; Preludes; Concerto for Flute
and Chamber Orchestra*
Paweł Bronkowski (flute), Polish Radio Grand Symphony
Orchestra, conducted by Jan Krenz. XL 0329

A rich selection of Polish works is also to be found on "Chronicle of the Warsaw Autumn" records from the years
1956—65.

VI. THE NEW VISAGE OF POLISH MUSIC

A Review of Events, Successes at Home and Abroad; A New Line-up; the Youngest Composers; Prominent Ensembles and Conductors; Festivals and Competitions; Organization of Music Life and Music Schools in Poland

The next watershed in the evolution of Polish music came in 1966 with the first world performance of Krzysztof Penderecki's *St. Luke Passion*. The consequences proved more momentous than could have been expected. This monumental work and the world-wide acclaim placed Penderecki among the most distinguished composers of our time. It also gave rise to numerous remonstrations among the extreme avant-garde. By accomplishing a synthesis of the great European musical tradition and contemporary achievements in the sphere of sound, Penderecki ceased to be the representative of the young and outré avant-garde he had been until then and became a classic of modern Polish music. Though the opposite of Witold Lutosławski as regards content and media, he rose to a place of equal importance and from then on Polish music began to revolve within the orbit of one or the other with a polarization in the views of critics and public: although these two utterly contrasting artists do not deliberately take opposite sides, their works have represented two different and well-nigh mutually exclusive music worlds. For other composers there arose the new problem of preserving their creative identity. If most of them have succeeded in doing so, none has so far managed to achieve similar popularity or international reputation. On the other hand the great worldwide success of these two has clearly been an impetus to a large group of composers, in particular among the younger generation: in the past few years there has been a noticeable intensification of creative work and accompanying efforts to enliven the various Polish festivals of contemporary music and give them more importance and standing. Persistent endeavours have also been made to arouse interest in modern music among the wider public.

A review of major events in the past few years shows no flagging in music life. The friendly observer will surely be pleased to note that artists, already well-known and recognized, have notched up further successes; what is particularly gratifying, however, is that from the multitude of dates, titles and names there is emerging a picture of a talented new generation to carry on the torch in the years to come.

Tadeusz Baird received the 1966 Award of the Polish Composers' Union, the Tribune des Compositeurs in Paris commended his *Dialogues* for oboe and chamber orchestra, and soon afterwards the Grand Theatre in Warsaw presented the first production of his opera, *Tomorrow*. Bolesław Szabelski was granted a State Award Class I. Romuald Twardowski won a competition organized on the 20th anniversary of the "Prague Spring" Festival. Works by Tomasz Sikorski, Bolesław Szabelski and Witold Szalonek were performed at the SIMC Festival in Stockholm. At the Malawski Competition, awards were won by Edward Bogusławski, Romuald Twardowski and Krystyna Moszumańska-Nazar, and the Fitelberg Competition drew attention to the talent of the young Bernadetta Matuszczak. In hindsight, however, all such developments pale in comparison with the world première of Krzysztof Penderecki's *St. Luke Passion* which took place in Münster Cathedral on 30 March 1966 and echoed loudly round the world. But though this great work made him an international name, he also found himself coming under fire from the extreme avant-garde. The Italian critic and musicologist Emilio Carapezza wrote:

The orthodox critics often accuse Penderecki of betraying his own avant-garde past. I consider this accusation completely unjust; it is to his experimental achievements that he owes his present power of dramatic expression. Moreover, I believe that his experimental past remains alive and present in such big dramatic forms as the *Passion* and *Dies Irae* and makes them so immensely absorbing. I, for one, admire this true evolution in Penderecki. It permitted him to give much more scope to his great inventiveness and avoid at the same time the danger of fossilization and stylization. (Ruch Muzyczny, No 4, 1969).

In the same year, 1966, the First International Festival of Old Music from Central and Eastern Europe was held in Bydgoszcz and opened the eyes of music historians setting on foot a re-consideration of standard views of the history of European music.

In the performing arts, 1966 brought a sensational triumph for a young Polish violinist, Andrzej Konstanty Kulka, at the competition in Munich (1st prize) and the first step to a rapid worldwide career. At the competition in Geneva, the trombonist Roman Siwek was awarded 1st prize in his class and the pianist and composer Zygmunt Krauze won 1st prize at the competition for interpreting contemporary music in Utrecht.

The year 1967 again put Witold Lutosławski in the news when he received the coveted Léonie Sonning Award "in recognition and admiration of his masterly compositional virtuosity which is a source of inspiration to the musical life of our times". Soon afterwards, he presented in Katowice the first performance of his magnificent *2nd Symphony* which subsequently became the highlight of the "Warsaw Autumn" Festival. The annual award of the Polish Composers' Union went for the second time to Bolesław Szabelski. At the Fitelberg Competition, prizes were won by Piotr Warzecha, Romuald Twardowski and Krzysztof Meyer. The Tribune des Compositeurs honoured works by two young composers: Henryk M. Górecki's *Refrain* and Zbigniew Bujarski's *Contraria*. The annual Festival of Contemporary Music in Cheltenham, England, presented music by Bacewicz, Górecki, Lutosławski, Penderecki and Serocki. Polish works were performed at the Biennale in Zagreb (Baird, Dobrowolski), at the SIMC Festival in Prague (Zbigniew Rudziński), in Stockholm (first performance of Serocki's *Continuum*), in Paris (first performance of Bogusławski's *Intonations II*), as well as in Japan, the United States, Brazil, and elsewhere.

Young performers also achieved successes: at the 5th Wieniawski Violin Competition, Piotr Janowski was awarded 1st prize, though, it must be said, the competition was not particularly stiff. At the competition in Toulouse, 1st prize went to Zdzisława Donat (singing), and at the competition in Geneva to Jerzy Sulikowski (piano). The singers Jadwiga Gadulanka and Zdzisław Krzywicki collected 2nd prizes at Munich and Toulouse, respectively.

The greatest success of Polish music in 1968 was the

presentation of the Koussevitzky Award to Tadeusz Baird "for outstanding contributions to the music of our times"; soon afterwards, Baird confirmed this accolade with the first performance in Rotterdam of his excellent *Sinfonia brevis*. The Tribune des Compositeurs awarded 1st prize to Lutosławski's *2nd Symphony* and that same year he presented in Hagen his next work: *Livre pour orchestre*. In Monaco, Romuald Twardowski received a special distinction for *Little Orthodox Liturgy* for vocal ensemble and three groups of instruments. The young Ryszard Kwiatkowski won a prize at a competition in Buffalo for his *Quartet for Percussion*, and with Krzysztof Meyer and Juliusz Łuciuk shared the honours at the Fitelberg Competition. At the Malawski Competition, awards went to Marek Stachowski, Jerzy Maksymiuk and Witold Szalonek. A State Award Class I was awarded to Krzysztof Penderecki for *Dies irae*. The 12th "Warsaw Autumn" and the annual SIMC Festival, held in Warsaw that year, brought several first performances, including Bolesław Szabelski's remarkable *5th Symphony*. Polish music was played in Leningrad, Dijon, Ghent, Havana, Mexico, Madrid, etc.

There was also another series of triumphs for young performers: two 1st prizes in Vercelli went to Aleksandra Ablewicz (piano) and Elżbieta Chojnacka (harpsichord), and the 1st prize in Graz to Teresa May-Czyżowska (singing); 2nd prizes were won in Naples by Ewa Osińska (piano), in Barcelona by Ewa Synowiec (piano), in Toulouse by Ryszard Arning (singing); the pianist Piotr Paleczny won 3rd prize in Munich.

The most important event of 1969 was unquestionably the world première in Hamburg of Krzysztof Penderecki's first opera the *Devils of Loudun*. The programme of the SIMC Festival, which took place in Hamburg at the same time, contained a record number of works by Polish composers: Tadeusz Baird, Henryk Górecki, Bernadetta Matuszczak, Kazimierz Serocki and Witold Szalonek. In the same year, Witold Lutosławski made a concert tour of Holland, Norway and Austria where he conducted performances of his own works; he was also elected an honorary member of SIMC. Włodzimierz Kotoński lectured at the Swedish Academy of Music. Romuald Twardowski's popularity also increased; together with Marek Stachowski, he won a prize at the competition in Skopje, and his works were performed in France, Spain, Denmark and other countries. Another young Polish composer, Joanna Bruzdowicz, achieved her first success in Paris. At home, the Fitelberg Competition brought laurels to Jerzy Maksymiuk, Jan Fotek, Piotr Warzecha and Tadeusz Natanson, demonstrating that the vanguard of the youngest composers had not taken shape fortuitously.

In 1969 performers fared less well; but, for the record, violinist Kaja Danczowska was awarded 2nd prize at the competition in Naples, Andrzej Kalarus (double-bass) 2nd prize at the competition in Munich, and violinist Robert Szreder 3rd prize at the competition for interpreting contemporary music in Utrecht.

The good run continued in 1970. The annual awards of the Polish Composers' Union went to Krzysztof Penderecki and Henryk M. Górecki. Tadeusz Baird received a State Award Class I and made a prolonged tour of Japan. The prize-winners in the Malawski Competition were Piotr Warzecha and Edward Bogusławski and in the Fitelberg Competition Przemysława Rzucidło and Anna Kamińska. Krzysztof Penderecki presented his *Utrenya* and was commissioned by the United Nations to compose a work for its 25th anniversary, *Cosmogony*, which was performed at a special function in New York. Witold Lutosławski produced his *Cello Concerto,* performed by Mstislav Rostropovich in London. Works by Andrzej Dobrowolski and Witold Lutosławski were included in the programme of the SIMC Festival in Basel. Krzysztof Meyer was granted the Rainier III Award in Monaco for the opera *Cyberiada.*

The "Music Workshop" and "MW-2" ensembles made a number of concert tours abroad, performing Polish avant-garde music. The 8th Chopin Piano Competition unearthed some talented young artists: Garrick Ohlsson from the United States (1st prize), Mitsuko Uchida from Japan (2nd), Piotr Paleczny from Poland (3rd), Eugene Indjic from the United States (4th), Natalia Gavrilova from the Soviet Union (5th) and Janusz Olejniczak from Poland (6th). In the same year, another Polish pianist, Andrzej Dutkiewicz was awarded 2nd prize at the competition in Rotterdam, the violinist Kaja Danczowska 2nd prize at the competition in Geneva, and the singer Bożena Betley 2nd prize at the competition in Toulouse.

Among the events of 1971, there was the granting of the Ravel and Académie Charles Cros Awards to Witold Lutosławski and the Jurzykowski Award to Tadeusz Baird. Works by Augustyn Bloch and Zbigniew Rudziński were performed at the SIMC Festival in London. Krzysztof Penderecki composed the second part of *Utrenya.* Polish music resounded from Zagreb and Barcelona to Cleveland and had become an integral part of contemporary musical culture.

Young Polish performers also attested to the high

standard of musical art in Poland: Bogumiła Reszke (cello) won 1st prize at the competition in Geneva, Ewa Bukojemska (piano) 2nd prize at the competition in Barcelona, Andrzej Mróz (singing) 2nd prize at the competition in Geneva, Antoni Wit (conducting) 2nd prize at the Karajan Competition in Berlin, and the young Wilanowski Quartet, 2nd prize at the competition for chamber ensembles in Vienna.

As we have said, the present line-up in music was fused in 1966. The composing world is now a variegated structure, dominated by the outstanding personalities of Witold Lutosławski and Krzysztof Penderecki. Lutosławski's oeuvre has been augmented by the *2nd Symphony* (1967), *Livre pour orchestre* (1968) and *Cello Concerto* (1970), written for the great Soviet cellist, Mstislav Rostropovich. In the past few years, he has been devoting more and more time to concert tours conducting his works.

Krzysztof Penderecki has recently also taken to conducting and has, for instance, made with the Polish Radio and TV Grand Symphony Orchestra for EMI two quadrofonic records which include some of his newest works: *Capriccio per violino e orchestra* (1967), *Prelude* for a brass band, percussion and double-bass (1971), *De natura sonoris II* for orchestra (1971), and *Partita* for harpsichord and orchestra (1972). Of others written in the past few years by this remarkably prolific composer, mention should be made of *De natura sonoris I* for orchestra (1966), *Dies irae* for solo voices, choir and orchestra (1967), *Pittsburgh Overture* for brass band and kettle-drums (1967), *Quartetto per archi II* (1968), the opera *The Devils of Loudun* (1969), *Cosmogony* for solo voices and orchestra (1970), *Utrenya* for solo voices, choir and orchestra (1971),

143

Actions for chamber ensemble (1971), *Carmina curat* for six men's voices (1972), and *Canticum canticorum* (1972). He received an honorary doctorate from the University of Rochester, was appointed Rector of the College of Music in Cracow, and lectured at Yale University.

In would be an obvious mistake, however, to allow the spotlight focussed on these two composers to push others into the wings. The honours and international tokens of recognition, which have been cited here only very summarily, pay eloquent tribute to the depth of quality in the Polish music world. Though demarcations according to style are bound to be self-defeating — if only because there are continual changes and surprises — there still exists a rough (but increasingly blurred) division into three groups, differing not so much in age as size and length of creative accomplishment.

The first group includes, apart from the above-mentioned leading duo, Bolesław Szabelski, Tadeusz Baird, Kazimierz Serocki, Włodzimierz Kotoński, Andrzej Dobrowolski, Zbigniew Wiszniewski, Witold Rudziński, Zbigniew Turski and Zygmunt Mycielski. From what has already been said about them, it will be clear that not only does each of them possess a distinctive persona, but also that there are great differences in their attitudes towards problems of technique, the avantgarde and the aestetics of contemporary music.

Of Tadeusz Baird's latest works the musical drama *Tomorrow* (1966), *Four Songs to Poems by Vesna Parun* (1966) *Four Short Stories* for chamber orchestra (1967) and *Five Songs to Poems by Halina Poświatowska* (1968) all represent the highly individual style hammered out in the late fifties and subsequently only elaborated upon and intensified. More recent compositions, however, seem to be evidence of an attempt to broaden this style's potential and mark a definite advance. They include *Sinfonia breve* for orchestra (1968), *3rd Symphony* (1969), the cantata *Goethe's Letters* (1970), *Play* for a string quartet (1971) and *Psychodrama* for orchestra (1972). A clue to his music can be found in what Baird said in an interview for Ruch Muzyczny (No. 6, 1971):

For me, music has been and, I hope, will continue to be a way of expressing emotions and feelings, the adventures of my life, adventures in the inner sphere, of course. And, from this point of view, what I have tried to write in the past 20 years might, in a certain sense, be called a scrapbook, an autobiography written down in sounds. Being in sounds, it is naturally fully legible only to me. All the same, this is probably the very thing, the extreme subjectivity of my compositions, that makes me dislike attending public performances of my works. I realize, of course, that the audience is unaware of this but I know that I am engaged in something I call privately a 'spiritual striptease', and it is not always a very pleasant feeling.

The older I get, the less satisfied I feel with music in what I call (privately again) its chemically pure shape, that is with purely instrumental music. Music's greatest strength lies in its ability to communicate feelings and emotional states by means of sounds. At its best, most beautiful and most significant, it does so with a power unmatched by any other art. So, at any rate, it seems to me as a musician. On the other hand, this is exactly what I consider to be a weakness, one that troubles me more and more as time goes by: though music is a powerful instrument for communicating certain messages, these are shapeless, vague and imprecise. More and more acutely, and more frequently, I find it impossible to communicate to the potential listener a concrete and unambiguous message by means of sounds alone. In this predicament the only answer is to rely on words. This is why literature has come to have an ever greater influence on my purely musical ventures.

145

Kazimierz Serocki's restless creative temperament has produced a number of very varied compositions: *Niobe*, a poem for two reciting voices, choir and orchestra (1966), *Forte e piano* for two pianos, choir and orchestra (1967), *Continuum* for percussion instruments (1966), *Poems* for soprano and chamber orchestra (1969), *Dramatic Story* for orchestra (1970), *Swinging Music* for instrumental ensemble (1970), *Phantasmagoria* for piano and percussion (1971) and *Fantasia elegiaca* for organ and orchestra (1972).

Another of this group, Grażyna Bacewicz, died in 1969, leaving uncompleted a ballet version of Pablo Picasso's *Desire Caught by the Tail*. Before that, she had composed *Contradizione* for chamber ensemble (1966) and *Concerto for Viola and Orchestra* (1967). Though she was always extremely reluctant to talk about her own music, an interesting piece of self-description, the draft of an answer to some poll, was found among her papers:

I have not crossed so far, and now never will, the line that separates us from 'the absurd'. In this case, by 'the absurd' I mean things that seem impossible but in fact yield completely new values. To give an example, I believe that Beckett crossed this line in *Waiting for Godot*: two fellows standing on a stage and just talking, about as un-theatrical as you can get, and yet the result is overwhelming. I tread the line that divides these two worlds. However, my present music, containing the specific element it does, unquestionably belongs to the avant-garde... I divide my music into three periods: one, youthful and very experimental; the second unjustly dubbed neo-classical while in fact atonal; and the third in which I am still stuck. I reached it by way of evolution (not revolution)... In my music, a great deal happens, it is aggressive and at the same time lyrical. Because I am anxious not to create additional difficulties for the performers, and because I do not like leaving anything to chance in music, I score my compositions in the traditional way, even passages bearing all the characteristics of aleatorism. This causes me a lot of trouble. There are, of course, problems or effects for 'which, there being no equivalent in the old notation, I have had to invent and employ one of my own.

Carrying on his creative interests, Włodzimierz Kotoński took charge of the Electronic Music Studio at the College of Music in Warsaw in 1967. In the same year, he composed *Sound Games* for controlled recording tape, followed by *Pour quatre* written for "Music Workshop" (1968), *Music for Sixteen Cymbals and Strings* (1969), the electronic *Aela and Euridice* (1970), *Multiplay* for six brass instruments: instrumental theatre (1971), and *Concerto per oboe* (1972).

Andrzej Dobrowolski produced *Music for Strings, Two Groups of Wind Instruments and Two Loudspeakers* (1967), *Music for Orchestra* (1968), *Krabogupa* for four instruments, written for "Music Workshop" (1969), *Music for Orchestra No. 2 — Amar* (1970), and *Music for Recording Tape and Piano* (1971).

Zbigniew Wiszniewski's output included *Kammermusic No. 1* (1967), *Kammermusik No. 2* (1967), *Concerto for Clarinet and Strings* (1968), and several electronic works.

The interests of the remaining composers in the first group went in entirely different direction. Witold Rudziński remained faithful to stage and programme music, composing the opera *Sulamith* (1965), the symphonic *Pictures from the Świętokrzyskie Mountains* (1965), and the oratorios, *Gaude Mater Polonia* (1966) and *Lipce* (1968); for some time now he has been working on an opera version of Władysław Reymont's epic novel, *The Peasants*. In between music for the theatre and cinema, Zbigniew Turski composed a radio opera, *Small Talk* (1966), and a ballet, *Titania and the*

Ass (1967). Zygmunt Mycielski's latest work includes *3rd Symphony* (1965) and *Chorale Preludes* for orchestra (1967).

In the second group come the composers who made their début in the fifties and are now reaching their peak.

The most original and inventive of them is undoubtedly Bogusław Schäffer, invariably and uncompromisingly committed to the extreme avant-garde, giving vent to bold views in trenchantly argued articles and — perhaps for this reason — not very popular with most of his colleagues. In the period in question, he has written *Visual Music* for any five performers (1968), *Concerto for Piano and Orchestra* (1969), *Synectics* for three performers (1970), *Contract* for three performers (1971), *Heraclitiana* for solo harp and stereo recording tape (1971), *Experimenta* for orchestra (1972), and other pieces.

Henryk M. Górecki composed a series of works under the common title of *Muzyczka* (Little Music), for various chamber groups of instruments, plus *Cantata* for organ (1968), *Old-Polish Music* for orchestra (1969), *Canticum graduum* for orchestra (1969), and *Ad matrem* for soprano, choir and orchestra (1971).

Apart from some excellent film scores, the most noteworthy works by Wojciech Kilar have been *Solenne* (Solemn Music) for 67 performers (1967), *Training 68* for four instruments (1967), *Upstairs-Downstairs* for orchestra and small choir (1971), *Prelude and Christmas Carol* for orchestra (1972).

Witold Szalonek's talents blossomed forth an unexpected degree in this period. He is discoverer of "combined sounds", i.e. the multi-sounds, characteristic in colour, that can be extracted from woodwinds and in many of his compositions has made use of this sound material, new to European music. Often performed abroad, they include *Mutazioni* for chamber orchestra (1966), *Proporzioni* for flute, viola and harp (1967), *Improvisations sonoristiques* for clarinet, trombone, cello and piano, written for "Music Workshop" (1968), *Aarhus Music* for five wind instruments (1970), *For Strings* (1971) and *Connections* for ten instruments (1972).

Augustyn Bloch has also advanced in the past few years to the very front rank. For the well-known Mime Theatre in Wrocław he composed a ballet, *Gilgamesh* (1967), followed by an opera, *Jephthah's Daughter* (1969), *Enfiando per orchestra* (1970), commissioned by the City of Bonn for the 200th anniversary of Beethoven's birth; and for his wife, the distinguished singer, Halina Łukomska, he wrote *Salmo gioioso per soprano e cinque fiati* (1970).

But for sheer number of awards and distinctions at various competitions, pride of place belongs to Romuald Twardowski, a composer with a wide range of interests, though somewhat chary of avant-garde ideas. Of his many works, mention is due to the ballet *The Naked Prince* (1960), *Antifone per tre gruppi d'orchestra* (1961), the opera *Cyrano de Bergerac* (1962), the ballet *The Sorcerer's Statues* (1963), the morality play *Tragedie, or the Story of John and Herod* (1965), *Trittico fiorentino* (1967), *Little Orthodox Liturgy* (1968) and the radio opera *The Fall of Father Suryn* (1969).

The third group, the youngest and very active, comprises, among others, Zbigniew Bargielski (b. 1937), Edward Bogusławski (b. 1940), Joanna Bruzdowicz, Jan W. Hawel (b. 1936), Zygmunt Krauze (b. 1938), Jerzy

Maksymiuk (b. 1939), Bernadetta Matuszczak, Krzysztof Meyer (b. 1943), Zbigniew Rudziński (b. 1935), Tomasz Sikorski (b. 1939), Piotr Warzecha (b. 1941). It is revealing that the tutor of most of them was Bolesław Szabelski. Though they are being performed at many international festivals, it is still too early even for a rough delineation of their characteristics. The most one can do is single out some of the more interesting works. These include *Intonazioni* for orchestra (1967) and *Concerto per oboe, oboe d'amore, corno inglese, musette e orchestra* (1968) by Edward Bogusławski; the operas *The Penal Colony* after the Kafka story (1968) and *The Trojans* after J.P. Sartre (1972), by Joanna Bruzdowicz, who has been working in Paris for the past few years; *Folk Music* for orchestra (1971) by Zygmunt Krauze, composer, pianist and leader of "Music Workshop". An interesting and versatile figure is Jerzy Maksymiuk, composer, pianist and conductor at the Grand Theatre in Warsaw. Krzysztof Meyer, a pupil of Penderecki, has to his name three interesting symphonies and the prize-winning opera, *Cyberiada,* Zbigniew Rudziński, *Contra fidem* for orchestra (1964) and *Requiem* for choir, recitation and orchestra (1971), and Bernadetta Matuszczak, the chamber ballet *Juliet and Romeo* (1968), produced at the Grand Theatre in Warsaw. These are all composers whose further careers will be worth careful attention. Although one can hardly yet predict which of them will come to be recognized in the next few years as leading representatives of contemporary music, the large and growing number of these names in itself augurs well for the future.

It also shows that Polish composers are not haunted by that spectre of a total crisis of art that is abroad

in the West. Their outlook is one of optimism, summed
up by Witold Lutosławski in his article "Reflexions
on the Future of Music" (Tygodnik Powszechny,
19 November 1972):

In music, the process of 'disintegration' has been going on
ever since Wagner wrote the first three bars of *Tristan und
Isolde*. ...No doubt neither Wagner himself, nor still more the
other first 'destroyers' and 'wreckers' like Chopin or Liszt,
anticipated that the disintegration of the conventions built
up over the centuries would in a few decades gather bewil-
dering momentum and eventually lead to something that
might, with many reservations, be called 'anti-music'. ...That
there has been a process of 'destruction' must seem indisputable to anyone who gives a moment's thought to the fortunes
of music from *Tristan und Isolde* down to punching a hole
in a wall by means of a piano pushed by a sufficient number of 'performers'. And yet the transformations occurring in
the sphere of musical language, and even in aesthetics itself,
are only one side of the history of music in the period under
discussion. The other consists of the works created, considered individually and in isolation from the historical context.
The fact that the old classical conventions have not been
replaced by any new one which managed to survive more
than ten or fifteen years has not prevented a number of
genuine masterpieces being written. This is not the contra-
diction it might appear. The value of a work of art is not
to be measured by the value of its underlying principles and
conventions alone, but is largely independent of them. It is
in fact the principles and conventions which are legitimized
by the value what they have been used for. A masterpiece
can be created by means of the most 'unconvincing' or even
absurd principles and conventions, whereas none, however
estimable in themselves, can redeem rubbish. This, of course,
immediately raised the question: what is rubbish and what
is a masterpiece? I take the view that there are no standards
of value in art. In each case, it depends on the feelings of
the listener, which elude objective and rational justification.
It is the sum total of the feelings of many thousands of li-
steners over the course of many decades, as symbolized by

the term 'time', which determines value. The past dozen or so decades prove this an astonishingly positive judgment. In spite of the 'process of disintegration' of the classical conventions, which has now reached the point of absurdity, musical works of indisputable merit and power have been continually appearing — overwhelming proof of the way that the frail and brittle substance of music is subordinated to the human spirit which altogether refuses to be sucked into the 'process of disintegration'. The power of this spirit, as manifested in man's works, makes me confident that the crisis in the substance of music, although alarmingly deep, is none the less temporary. The more freedom we give to the creation and circulation of the music written today, however 'radical', the sooner we can expect a revival of the substance of music. Artificial barriers can only delay the overcoming of the crisis. This process must follow its natural course. I am perfectly sure that it will be accomplished that art will not suffer self-destruction. It has been a need so passionately inherent in mankind from the beginning of its history, so essential an attribute of humanity, that I can only conceive the one disappearing with the other.

*

The busily thriving music life of Poland today is made up mainly of the concerts and stagings which fill out a season lasting from 1 September to 30 June, plus numerous festivals and competitions. In addition to Polish Radio and TV Symphony Orchestra which, apart from its radio broadcasts, also gives regular public concerts, there are 15 State Philharmonics (Bydgoszcz, Cracow, Gdańsk, Katowice, Kielce, Koszalin, Lublin, Łódź, Olsztyn, Opole, Poznań, Rzeszów, Szczecin, Warsaw, Wrocław) and 4 State Symphony orchestras (Białystok, Częstochowa, Poznań, Zielona Góra). The best is, of course, the world-famous National Philharmonic in Warsaw, directed by Witold Rowicki and Andrzej Markowski. In the past few years, a very high standard has also been attained by the Silesian Philharmonic in Katowice, headed since 1953 by Karol Stryja, and the Szymanowski Philharmonic in Cracow, now under Jerzy Katlewicz. Others worth mentioning are the Wrocław Philharmonic under Tadeusz Strugała, the Łódź Philharmonic under Henryk Czyż, and the Paderewski Pomeranian Philharmonic in Bydgoszcz under Witold Krzemieński. Interesting initiatives have also been undertaken recently by the State Symphony Orchestra in Zielona Góra and its present manager, the talented pianist and conductor, Kazimierz Morski.

None of these institutions, least of all the Philharmonics, confine themselves to the ordinary round of concerts. Supported and supervised by municipal authorities, they are well-equipped centres helping to promote the music life of their particular region, by organizing recitals of chamber and popular music, maintaining various choral and instrumental ensembles, sponsoring festivals, etc. For example there are excellent choirs at the National Philharmonic and the Szymanowski Philharmonic in Cracow. Others, which often collaborate with the Philharmonics, are the Polish Radio Choir in Wrocław, the Choir of the Szczecin Polytechnic under Jerzy Szyrocki, the famous Poznań Boys' Choir under Stefan Stuligrosz and the Boys' Choir under Jerzy Kurczewski, the latter two mainly performing old music.

Old music, which is enjoying increasing popularity, is also the province of the Chamber Orchestra of the National Philharmonic directed by Karol Teutsch; the "Capella Bydgostiensis pro Musica Antiqua", at the Pomeranian Philharmonic in Bydgoszcz formed by Stanisław Gałoński; the Madrigal Singers; and a number of other ensembles, such as "Con Moto ma Cantabile", organized and conducted by Tadeusz Ochlewski, or

"Fistulatores et Tubicinatores Varsovienses". The latter deserves particular attention: formed in 1964 by Kazimierz Piwkowski, it uses instruments built by him according to old Polish drawings, descriptions in treatises and models in museum collections. It has toured many European countries and Japan with its repertoire of Medieval, Renaissance and Baroque music and has also made several records.

At the opposite pole are two chamber ensembles specializing in avant-garde music which are already well known in the world: the Warsaw "Music Workshop" founded in 1963 by composer and pianist Zygmunt Krauze and at first associated with the Polish Radio Experimental Studio, and the Cracow "MW-2", directed by Adam Kaczyński and Marek Mietelski. Both groups have toured widely, played at numerous festivals and made a number of records.

The other mainstay of music life is provided by nine opera stages (Bydgoszcz, Bytom, Cracow, Gdańsk, Łódź, Poznań, Warsaw, Wrocław) and nine operetta companies (Cracow, Gdynia, Gliwice, Lublin, Łódź, Poznań, Szczecin, Warsaw, Wrocław). Like the Philharmonics and symphony orchestras, they are all municipal enterprises.

The shop-window is Warsaw's Grand Theatre, which has two auditoriums and the cream of the country's musicians, singers and dancers. In this role it has challengers in the Grand Theatre in Łódź and, until recently, the Moniuszko Opera in Poznań under the management of Robert Satanowski. The other musical theatres have somewhat lower standards and cater to more traditional tastes in their repertoire and productions. However, there are some which have broken out of this rut: the recently established Warsaw Chamber Opera, directed by Stefan Sutkowski, which is above all reviving old and little known pieces, and the Music Theatre in Gdynia where Danuta Baduszko is striving to build up a worthwhile Polish musical comedy repertoire.

Apart from the regular concerts and productions of Philharmonics, orchestras and music theatres, there is an abundance of international or national competitions and festivals devoted to all kinds of music and attracting big audiences. We have already repeatedly referred to the "Warsaw Autumn" International Festivals of Contemporary Music, traditionally inaugurated on the first Saturday after 15 September every year, the Frédéric Chopin International Piano Competitions held in Warsaw every five years (the next in 1975), and the Henryk Wieniawski International Violin Competitions, organized every five years in Poznań (the next in 1977).

These three are the best known events, but to them should be added the International Festivals of Old Music of Central and Eastern Europe, held in Bydgoszcz in September every three years (the 4th Festival to take place in 1975), and the "Wratislavia Cantans" International Oratorio and Cantata Festival, initiated and directed by Andrzej Markowski in Wrocław, held every August. Furthermore there is an International Festival of Russian and Soviet Music in Katowice in November every three or four years which acquaints audiences with the most important classics and the latest achievements of Soviet music. It last took place in 1972.

In a wholly different vein an annual International Song Festival and International "Jazz Jamboree" have been organized for a number of years in Sopot and Warsaw, in August and October respectively.

Among domestic events devoted to contemporary music the most important are the National Festivals of Contemporary Music in Wrocław, organized in February every other year, and the annual "Poznań Musical Spring" in April. Both are a review of contemporary Polish works and a sort of complement to the "Warsaw Autumn".

Old music is presented at the annual "Organ Music Days" in Cracow (March), "Days of Old Masters' Music" and "Organ and Harpsichord Music Days" in Wrocław (April), "Chamber Music Days" (May) at the chateau in Łańcut, and two summer events of longer standing, the Festival of Organ Music in Gdańsk-Oliwa and the Festival of Organ and Chamber Music in Kamień Pomorski, both of which places have the advantage of possessing magnificent old organs. A Bydgoszcz Music Festival is held annually in September and every third year becomes the above-mentioned international event.

To these we can add the monographic Moniuszko Festivals at Kudowa (July) and the traditional Chopin Festivals at Duszniki (August) and a number of others best described by their names: the Polish Piano Festivals in Słupsk, which have gained wide popularity, the Choral Song Festivals at Świnoujście (July), the Grażyna Bacewicz Polish Violin Festivals in Częstochowa (March) and the annual Competitions in Piano Improvisation in Gdańsk (April). For the young there are the "Pro Musica" Festivals in Częstochowa (November), organized by the Polish Section of "Jeunesses Musicales" and the Young Musicians' Festivals in Gdańsk. In addition there are several jazz and song festivals every year, the most important being "Jazz on the Odra" in Wrocław (March) and the Festival of Polish Song in Opole (July).

Supervisory and co-ordinating functions in the organization of music life in Poland are vested in the Department of Music at the Ministry of Culture and Art, whose Purchasing and Grants Commission, comprising composers and representatives of musical organizations is the practical embodiment of state patronage. Its Bureau for Cultural Cooperation with Other Countries looks after the maintaining and development of international music contacts.

As regards the organization of concert life, the main role belongs to the "Pagart" Polish Artistic Agency which is Poland's only concert agency, organizing appearances of foreign artists in Poland and cooperating in the organization of Polish artists' appearances abroad.

Polish musicians have three professional organizations: composers belong to the Polish Composers' Union and/or to the Union of Light Music Authors and Composers; performers to the Polish Musicians' Association. In addition, all creative artists may belong to the "Zaiks" Authors' Association whose task is to protect copyright and collect royalties.

Other vigorous organizations are the Frédéric Chopin Society, the Henryk Wieniawski Poznań Music Society, the Stanisław Moniuszko Warsaw Music Society and the Polish Section of "Jeunesses Musicales".

In the publishing field, the Polish Music Press in Cracow is the most important and virtually the only institution. The music press is represented by the informative fortnightly review Ruch Muzyczny, the quarterly Muzyka, devoted to the history and theory of music, and the monthly Jazz. Records are produced by "Polskie Nagrania".

Music education in Poland has a three-tier structure

running from elementary and secondary schools (both providing a general education as well) to colleges of music (in Cracow, Katowice, Łódź, Poznań, Sopot, Warsaw and Wrocław). The latter have, as a rule, five departments: composition, theory and conducting; instrumental; vocal; teaching; and direction.

*

In Poland today, music is flourishing in every respect, both in the quantitative and qualitative sense. Our musical culture is growing and getting richer, the number of talented and highly qualified artists is increasing. At the same time, however, the public demand is also increasing. Polish musicians are aware of the fact that it has been granted to them to live in a period the like of which Polish musical culture has never known before. Still present, however, is that feeling of creative discontent, that unsatisfied hunger, that striving after ever-elusive perfection — which are the motive power of evolution and progress in art. Seeing our musicians, by no means sated with their accomplishments and success, restless, not unfrequently at variance with one another — one can look with confidence into the future of Polish music.

RECORDINGS BY "POLSKIE NAGRANIA — MUZA" OF
NEWEST POLISH MUSIC (selection)

Grażyna Bacewicz: *Concerto for Viola and Orchestra; Concerto for Two Pianos and Orchestra; In una parte*
Stefan Kamasa (viola), Jerzy Maksymiuk and Jerzy Witkowski (pianos), Symphony Orchestra of the National Philharmonic, conducted by Stanisław Wisłocki. XL 0875

Tadeusz Baird: *Four Songs to Poems by Vesna Parun* for mezzo-soprano and chamber orchestra; *Four Short Stories* for chamber orchestra
Krystyna Szostek-Radkowa (mezzo-soprano), Symphony Orchestra of the National Philharmonic, conducted by Witold Rowicki. XL 0562

Tadeusz Baird: *3rd Symphony*
Symphony Orchestra of the National Philharmonic, conducted by Jan Krenz. XL 0571

Andrzej Dobrowolski: *Krabogapa*
The "Musical Workshop" Ensemble. XL 0573

Henryk M. Górecki: *Old-Polish Music* for orchestra
Symphony Orchestra of the National Philharmonic, conducted by Andrzej Markowski. XL 0547

Włodzimierz Kotoński: *Pour quatre*
The "Musical Workshop" Ensemble. XL 0573

Zygmunt Krauze: *Polychromies*
The "Musical Workshop" Ensemble. XL 0573

Witold Lutosławski: *2nd Symphony*
Symphony Orchestra of the National Philharmonic, conducted by Witold Lutosławski. XL 0453

Witold Lutosławski: *Livre pour orchestre*
Symphony Orchestra of the National Philharmonic, conducted by Jan Krenz. XL 0571

159

Krzysztof Penderecki: *Dies irae; Polymorphia; De natura sonoris I*
Stefania Woytowicz (soprano), Wiesław Ochman (tenor), Bernard Ładysz (bass), Choir and Orchestra of the Cracow Philharmonic, conducted by Henryk Czyż. XL 0413

Krzysztof Penderecki: *Utrenya* (I. *Deposition of Christ to the Tomb*, II. *Resurrection)*
Soloists, Choir and Symphony Orchestra of the National Philharmonic, conducted by Andrzej Markowski. XL 0889

Zbigniew Rudziński: *Moments Musicaux for Orchestra*
Symphony Orchestra of the National Philharmonic, conducted by Witold Rowicki. XL 0336

Kazimierz Serocki: *Swinging Music*
The "Musical Workshop" Ensemble. XL 0573

Bolesław Szabelski: *5th Symphony*
Symphony Orchestra of the National Philharmonic, conducted by Andrzej Markowski. XL 0547

Witold Szalonek: *Improvisations sonoristiques*
The "Musical Workshop" Ensemble. XL 0573

Romuald Twardowski: *Little Orthodox Liturgy; Tre studi secondo Giotto*
Soloists, "Capella Bydgostiensis", conducted by Stanisław Gałoński. XL 0592

A wide selection of new Polish works is also to be found on the "Chronicle of the Warsaw Autumn" records of the past few years.

FOREIGN RECORDINGS OF CONTEMPORARY POLISH MUSIC (selection)

Grażyna Bacewicz: *Music for Strings, Trumpets and Percussion*
Symphony Orchestra of the National Philharmonic, conducted by Witold Rowicki. Philips 839260 DSY

Tadeusz Baird: *Erotiques* for soprano and orchestra
Stefania Woytowicz (soprano), Symphony Orchestra of the National Philharmonic, conducted by Witold Rowicki. Philips 839260 DSY

Tadeusz Baird: *Four Essays* for orchestra; *Espressioni* for violin and orchestra: *Variations Without Theme* for orchestra
Wanda Wiłkomirska (violin), Symphony Orchestra of the National Philharmonic, conducted by Witold Rowicki. Philips 835265 AY

Andrzej Dobrowolski: *Music for Recording Tape and Solo Oboe*
Janusz Banaszek (oboe), tape recorded at the Experimental Studio of the Polish Radio. Philips 6740001

Henryk Mikołaj Górecki: *Monologhi per soprano and tre gruppi di strumenti*
Joan Carroll (soprano), Gustav Scheck (flute), Ensemble für neue Musik, conducted by Arghyris Kounadis. Wergo 60056

Włodzimierz Kotoński: *Microstructures* (musique concrète)
Tape recorded at the Experimental Studio of the Polish Radio. Philips 6740001

Witold Lutosławski: *Variations on a Theme of Paganini* for two pianos
Bracha Eden and Alexander Tamir, pianos. Decca SXL 6158
Vitya Vronsky and Victor Babin (pianos). His Master's Voice Alp-2065 Asc-614
V. and V. Lejsek (pianos). Supraphon SUA ST 50694

Witold Lutosławski: *Little Suite*, *Overture* for strings, *Five Dance Preludes, Straw Chainlet, Musique Funèbre*
Berliner Symphonie Orchester, conducted by Arthur Grüber, Barbara Müller (soprano), Oksana Sowiak (mezzo-soprano), Joseph Masseli (clarinet). Candide-Vox CE 31035

Witold Lutosławski: *Concerto for Orchestra*
Orchestre de la Suisse Romande, conducted by Paul Kletzki. Decca SXL 644
Chicago Symphony Orchestra, conducted by Seji Ozawa. Electrola 1 C 063-02118

Witold Lutosławski: *Musique Funèbre, Concerto for Orchestra, Jeux Vénitiens* for orchestra
Symphony Orchestra of the National Philharmonic, conducted by Witold Rowicki. Philips 839261 DSY

Witold Lutosławski: *String Quartet*
LaSalle String Quartet. Deutsche Grammophon 137001
LaSalle String Quartet. Wergo 60019

Witold Lutosławski: *Postlude, Trois Poèmes d'Henri Michaux*
Polish Radio Grand Symphony Orchestra, Choir of the Polish Radio in Cracow, conducted by Jan Krenz and Witold Lutosławski. Wergo 60019

Witold Lutosławski: *1st Symphony, 2nd Symphony*
Polish Radio Grand Symphony Orchestra, conducted by Jan Krenz. Südwestfunkorchester Baden-Baden, conducted by Ernest Bour. Wergo 60044

Krzysztof Penderecki: album "Penderecki dirigiert Penderecki" *Fonogrami per flauto e orchestra da camera, Concerto per violoncello e orchestra, De natura sonoris no 2, Canon* for strings and recording tape, *Capriccio per violino e orchestra, Emanations* for two string orchestras, *Partita* for harpsichord and orchestra
Siegfried Palm (cello), Wanda Wiłkomirska (violin), Felicja Blumental (harpsichord), Polish Radio Grand Symphony Orchestra, conducted by the composer. Electrola C 193-02386/7

Krzysztof Penderecki: *1st Symphony, Anaclasis* for percussion and string orchestra
London Symphony Orchestra, conducted by Krzysztof Penderecki. Electrola SHZE 393

Krzysztof Penderecki: *Actions* for jazz band
The New Eternal Rhythm Orchestra, conducted by Krzysztof Penderecki. Philips 6305153

Krzysztof Penderecki: *St. Luke Passion*
Stefania Woytowicz (soprano), Andrzej Hiolski (baritone), Bernard Ladysz (bass), Leszek Herdegen (recitation), Choir and Orchestra of the Cracow Philharmonic, conducted by Henryk Czyż. Philips 802771/72 AY

Krzysztof Penderecki: *Devils of Loudun,* three-act opera
Tatiana Troyanos (Joan), Andrzej Hiolski (Grandier), Bernard Ladysz (Barré), Helmut Melchert (Laubardemont), Kurt Marschner (Adam), Heinz Blankenburg (Mannoury), Hamburg Staatsoper Orchestra and Choir, conducted by Marek Janowski. Philips 6700042

Krzysztof Penderecki: *Utrenya* for two choirs, solo voices and symphony orchestra
Stefania Woytowicz (soprano), Kerstin Meyer (mezzo-soprano), Seth McCoy (tenor), Bernard Ladysz (bass) and Peter Lagger (bass), Temple University Choir, Philadelphia Orchestra, conducted by Eugene Ormandy. RCA LSC 3180

Krzysztof Penderecki: *Threnody for the Victims of Hiroshima* for 52 string instruments
Symphony Orchestra of the National Philharmonic, conducted by Witold Rowicki. Philips 839260 DSY, Philips A 02382 L
Orchestra Sinfonica di Roma, conducted by Bruno Maderna. RCA VICS-1239, RCA 94004

Krzysztof Penderecki: *Quartetto per archi I*
LaSalle String Quartet. Deutsche Grammophon 137001

Krzysztof Penderecki: *Ecloga VIII* for six male voices
Schola Cantorum, Stuttgart, conducted by Clytus Gottwald. Wergo 60070

Kazimierz Serocki: *Sinfonietta* for two string orchestras
Symphony Orchestra of the National Philharmonic, conducted by Witold Rowicki. Philips 839260 DSY

Kazimierz Serocki: *Episodes* for strings and percussion,
Musica concertante for chamber orchestra, *Segmenti* for chamber ensemble, *Symphonic Frescoes for Orchestra*
Polish Radio Grand Symphony Orchestra, conducted by Jan Krenz. Wergo 60018

Kazimierz Serocki: *Episodes for strings and percussion,*
Les Percussions de Strasbourg. Philips 836992 DSY

Bogusław Schäffer: *Symphonie* (electronic music)
Tape recorded at the Experimental Studio of the Polish Radio.
Philips 6740001

Michał Spisak: *Hymne Olympique*
Monte-Carlo Choir and Orchestra, conducted by André Jouve. Ducretet-Thomson 470 C 097